Library Services
for Immigrants
and New Americans

LIBRARY SERVICES FOR IMMIGRANTS AND NEW AMERICANS

Celebration and Integration

Jennifer Koerber

LIBRARIES UNLIMITED™

An Imprint of ABC-CLIO, LLC

Santa Barbara, California • Denver, Colorado

Library of Congress Cataloging in Publication Control Number: 2017061528

ISBN: 978-1-4408-5877-2 (paperback)
      978-1-4408-5878-9 (ebook)

22 21 20 19 18   1 2 3 4 5

This book is also available as an eBook.

Libraries Unlimited
An Imprint of ABC-CLIO, LLC

ABC-CLIO, LLC
130 Cremona Drive, P.O. Box 1911
Santa Barbara, California 93116-1911
www.abc-clio.com

This book is printed on acid-free paper ∞

Manufactured in the United States of America

This book was inspired by articles written for *Library Journal*, and my research findings for those articles were the foundation for several chapters in this book. Specifically, Chapter 5: Workforce Development draws heavily upon the article "Working Toward Change," published in *Library Journal* on September 1, 2016. Quotes from "Celebration and Integration"—published in *Library Journal* on June 13, 2016—are included throughout the book.

CONTENTS

PREFACE

As I began writing this book, the political environment in the United States was shifting dramatically: President Barack Obama's term was ending and Donald Trump's was beginning. It was obvious from the presidential campaign that candidate Trump's views on immigrants and refugees were radically different from President Obama's, and the first months of Trump's term saw an immediate attack on these populations in the form of a travel ban from seven predominantly Muslim countries and new calls for a "wall" along the U.S. border with Mexico. These efforts have only rallied pro-diversity groups to push back harder and harder each time, but the chaos of this administration has disrupted tens of thousands of lives, ratcheting what was an undercurrent of uncertainty up to constant fears of arrest and deportation.

Possibly foolishly, I expected that by the time I submitted the manuscript, the change would have settled down to a predictable path that libraries could adapt to. Instead, the situation is as jumbled now as it was at the beginning, a different plot twist occurring almost weekly and renewed resistance with each turn. As I submitted the manuscript, the administration was pushing to revoke Deferred Action for Child Arrivals (DACA) status for nearly a million people who have only ever known the United States as home, a move that will destabilize hundreds of thousands of lives and the economies of cities and towns across the country.

How can libraries address this ever-changing situation through pro-grams and services? When speaking with Vicki Oatis, director of Youth Library Services at the Norwalk (CT) Public Library, I said, "There's no cookie cutter answer, no 'everyone should be doing XYZ.'" Vicki replied, "Right. We concentrate on the other things we *could* be doing, but books like this make us think, keep us on our toes." I hope that this book sug-gests a palette of ideas, perhaps to develop a running list of "what could we do" possibilities that would let you quickly respond to a grant applica-tion or partnership opportunity.

ACKNOWLEDGMENTS

First and foremost, thank you to everyone who worked with me during the course of writing this book. Speaking with so many impassioned library staff around the country reminded me again and again why I was doing this: that I wanted to tell the stories you are all too busy being awesome to tell.

Profound thanks to everyone who took the time to reply to my lengthy queries in person, on the phone, and via many emails:

- Boston Public Library: David Leonard
- Boise Public Library: Sarah Kelley-Chase, Joan Vestal, Renee Addington, Kathleen Stalder
- Brooklyn Public Library: Eva Raison
- Buffalo & Erie County Public Library: Dawn Peters, Mary Jean Jakubowski
- Carson City Library: Diane Baker
- Cedar Falls Public Library: Sheryl McGovern, Erin Thompson
- Fresno County Public Library: Michelle Gordon
- Grandview Heights Public Library: Canaan Faulkner
- Hartford Public Library: Homa Naficy

- Houston Public Library: MyTesha Tates
- Los Angeles Public Library: Alicia Moguel, Maddy Ildefonso
- Louisville Public Library: Sophie Maier
- Norwalk Public Library: Vicki Oatis
- Philadelphia Public Library: Niema Nelson
- Providence Public Library/RIFLI: Karisa Tashjian
- Rochester Hills Public Library: Michelle Wisniewski
- San Diego Public Library: Adriana (Ady) Huertes
- San José Public Library: Jill Bourne, Cris Johnson
- Schaumburg Township District Library: Helen Stewart
- Somerville Public Library: Glenn Ferdman, Cathy Piantigini
- Skokie Public Library: Amy Koester
- Topeka & Shawnee County Public Library: Marie Pyko

Thanks also to Kate Cunningham (Louisville), Moina Noor and Sharon Baanante (Norwalk), and Dr. Elena Izraeli (Rochester Hills), both for working with me and the amazing work they're doing at and with their local libraries. My geeky thanks to Jeremy Greybill (Multnomah PL) for his perfectly technical explanation of Drupal translation integration. Heartfelt appreciation and thanks to Mike Journee of the Office of the Mayor in Boise for not only talking about libraries with enthusiasm, but showing a deep knowledge of what it means to be a 21st-century library. Thanks to Annette Mattei and Meg Shope Koppel for their work on the Philadelphia Free Public Library's Paschalville Project; to Victoria Nielsen for her work leading New York's Immigrant Justice Corps; and to Commissioner Gregg Bishop of the New York Department of Small Business Services for all he's done to support immigrant entrepreneurs.

Professionally, so many thank yous to Barbara Ittner, my editor at Libraries Unlimited, for reaching out to me after reading the *Library Journal* article I wrote that inspired this book; and to Meredith Schwartz, my editor at *Library Journal*, who has been a stalwart supporter of my library journalism from the start. Also, to Michael Sauers, my occasional co-conspirator, who first convinced me I had the chops to write something like this.

More personally, thank you to my primary support network: Ry; Jess; Wendy; the greater Camberville socialsphere; and my crazy cat family of Foo, Kizzy, and Jinx. Y'all have kept me grounded and on course, inspired to do this as my social justice action while you engaged with yours.

Finally, and always, to Matt, for being my first and best critic, my rubber-duck debugging partner, and an all-around mensch who still makes better scrambled eggs than I do. Fifteen and twenty and many more . . .

INTRODUCTION

The goal of this book is to be a practical inspiration for libraries seeking to create or expand services to immigrants, refugees, and new Americans, regardless of their citizenship status. You can read it straight through and follow a natural progression of programs and services or dip in and out to address needs you've already identified in your community.

Throughout, you'll find quotes and examples from libraries large and small, from coastal cities to the heart of the plains and deep in the South. Libraries across the country are facing the challenges of serving newcomer populations, and many have found ingenious ways to do so. Each chapter also includes lists of resources and Brainstorm Boxes: ideas that came up during conversations with library staff but that haven't necessarily been done anywhere . . . yet.

Chapter 1 provides a history and overview of the waves of immigration to the United States, how libraries have responded to these newcomers over time, definitions of immigration terminology, and a look at current events as of the time of writing. We'll also address the idea of "sanctuary cities" and what that term has meant from its inception in the 1980s to its current implications.

Chapters 2 through 6 explore the major categories that programs and services to newcomers fall into in an order that reflects how directly they can have an impact on these populations or how straightforward they are for a library to implement. Each chapter describes a wide variety of programs and services, with examples from libraries across the country serving communities large and small.

In Chapter 2, we begin with an overall look at making library buildings and websites more accessible to speakers of dozens of languages and cultures; then Chapter 3 examines different approaches to English-language literacy efforts. Chapter 4 discusses how libraries can aid newcomers along the path to citizenship, from making information available to directly providing legal aid during the naturalization process. Chapter 5 zeroes in on how workforce development and job services at libraries can be targeted to assist immigrants and refugees with their specific needs. Chapter 6 shifts from ways that libraries can help newcomers integrate into their receiving communities to cultural celebrations and sharing programs.

With Chapter 7, we move away from direct service to related topics. In that chapter, we'll look at ways libraries can facilitate community building through outreach, partnerships, and conversations. More so than for other library efforts, initiatives intended to serve immigrants and refugees blend those three elements in nearly every interaction; it's a complex dance that can seem daunting, but when it works, the results increase exponentially.

Finally, Chapter 8 addresses ways to initiate and expand programs via promotion, data-driven evidence, and funding. We'll look at word of mouth and traditional marketing avenues, data gathering and outcomes measurement, funding possibilities, and how to maximize the budgets you do (or don't) have.

In every chapter, my focus is on the *how* of offering programs and services. The why is relatively straightforward: immigrants, refugees, and new citizens are members of our communities who are as entitled to library service as residents who can trace their families back generations. Unlike long-term residents, the newcomers' diversity of language, culture, and familiarity with life in the United States makes providing these programs and services more complex. Let's see what we can learn from libraries around the country who are doing this excellent work and where we can all go next.

1

◇ ◇ ◇

IMMIGRANTS AND REFUGEES
IN THE UNITED STATES
(AND LIBRARIES)

As long as libraries have been "free to all"—as the front of the Boston Public Library proudly proclaims—they have provided some kind of service to newcomers to this country. What has changed is the diversity of the countries of origin of the people we serve. Largely European or East Asian at the beginning of the 1900s, immigrants to the United States now come from every single country in the world, often with multiple languages and cultures from each.

As the United States rides the technological advancements of the 20th century to an education- and language-based culture, newcomers have more need of assistance to help integrate: just finding a job and navigating healthcare requires stronger language proficiency and understanding of bureaucracy than many arrive with. Libraries have risen to meet these needs with an ever-changing range of programs and services.

This chapter reviews the major waves of immigration to the United States over the past century, especially in some of the cities mentioned here. It addresses the idea of "sanctuary cities," which have a much longer history than suggested by current events, and defines the terms and acronyms used throughout the book. Last, it explores the barriers to library use that newcomers face and outlines the elements of immigrant integration.

WAVES OF IMMIGRATION

Before the late 1800s, the vast majority of Americans arrived from Europe or from Africa (by way of the Caribbean). There was less of sense of being an "immigrant" because *everyone* had arrived from somewhere else. It's only as multiple generations of families were born in the same place that the United States began to develop the sense of "not from here" that had existed in other countries for centuries. By the late 19th century, immigration had become a formal process with intake centers in large cities on the coasts and along major waterways.

Early 20th-Century Immigration

There have always been immigrants arriving from around the world, but in this brief overview, we'll generalize to highlight the changes. From the late 1800s through the early 1950s, immigrants to the United States largely came from two places: Europeans headed to the East Coast and Asians headed to the West Coast. Ellis Island in New York, one of the most iconic immigration intake stations, was active from 1892–1954, funneling newcomers through New York and out to the rest of the country.

As such, the New York Public Library (NYPL) was an early testing ground for services to immigrants and responded predominantly with language learning programs. An NYPL advertisement from 1920—in Hungarian—encourages newcomers to attend English language classes at the Tompkins Square branch.

Immigration dipped and soared during the world wars, and the floodgates opened for a last push as Europeans fleeing their devastated countries came to the United States, where jobs were plentiful as women left the workplace to become the housewives of the 1950s. Over the next 20 years, federal legislation both barred and extended welcomes to newcomers based on country of origin, with annual immigration quotas as low as 100 (people) from India and The Philippines to an influx of hundreds of thousands of refugees from political upheavals in Hungary, Korea, and Cuba.

In 1965, Lyndon Johnson signed the Hart-Celler Act, which replaced country-of-origin quotas with preferential categories based on family relationships and job skills, especially for occupations deemed critical by the U.S. Department of Labor. Whatever the intent of the act, it opened a pathway to immigrants and refugees from around the globe. Fifteen years later, the United States Refugee Act of 1980 provided a "permanent and systemic process" for refugees from all countries and provided "comprehensive and uniform provisions for the effective resettlement and absorption of those refugees who are admitted" (Refugee Act of 1980).

A Tale of Two Cities: Louisville, Kentucky, and Boise, Idaho

The next 40 years saw a radical increase in the diversity of newcomers to the United States. Air travel shifted the points of entry from large port cities like New York and San Francisco to cities throughout the interior, like Boise and Louisville. Arriving immigrant and refugee resettlement efforts also bypassed the "full" larger cities and sent newcomers to smaller cities and highly developed suburbs, where there was more space and—hopefully—better opportunities in the local economy.

"Idaho entered the refugee resettlement arena in 1975 when Governor John Evans established the Indochinese Refugee Assistance Program in response to the need for all states to participate in the resettlement of refugees fleeing the overthrow of U.S. supported governments in Southeast Asia" (Idaho Office of Refugees n.d.). Most of these newcomers were resettled in and around Boise and Twin Falls, Idaho's two largest cities. The first wave of refugees comprised people from Vietnam, Cambodia, and Laos, but they were joined in the 1980s by Eastern Europeans fleeing Soviet rule and religious oppression. By the 1990s, the countries of origin had shifted to include more than 2,500 refugees from Bosnia and Herzegovina and another 2,500 from other European countries, Africa, East Asia, the Near East, Central Asia, and the Caribbean. The 2000s have seen recent arrivals from Iraq, Congo, Burma, Bhutan, Afghanistan, and Somalia (Idaho Office of Refugees n.d.).

In Louisville, Kentucky, the story is similar, but with an added twist. Sophie Maier, Immigrant Services Librarian at the Iroquois Branch of the Louisville Free Public Library, is a long-time resident of the city who has seen the change firsthand. "In the Seventies and Eighties, we were very black and white, with a very small number of people of Spanish-speaking descent. In the late Eighties, we got a community of Vietnamese folks through refugee resettlement. In the mid- to late-Nineties, both of our refugee resettlement agencies became very popular internationally because we were very successful. It started through the era of Bosnian, Sudanese, Rwandan refugees and just grew and grew and grew." At the same time, construction at the Churchill Downs Racetrack (home of the Kentucky Derby) brought a small uptick in Spanish speakers, though not as significant at those in comparable cities. "Our [newcomers were] much more diverse because of the whole nature of refugee resettlement: you don't know who you're getting year to year. Even within a single country's refugee community, you have all the different ethnic minorities and all those different languages. That's how it's added up so fast here" (Maier 2017).

Sophie adds that many in the city, especially younger or more afflu-ent residents, don't know about this rich history. "That's where the value of the outreach librarian comes in . . . These kids [from a nearby private university] have no idea because we're also a very segregated city, so those who live in the white wealthy neighborhoods are going to be the ones least likely to know about this diversity. Our Cultural Showcases spotlight that, but also going out and spreading the word is super-important." Sophie's efforts are examples we'll look at through-out the book.

"Cities and States of Refuge for the Oppressed"

One term that is widely used, but not universally understood or agreed on, is "sanctuary city" or "TRUST Act city." This language has been in use since the early 1980s in response to the dramatic changes in country of origin for newcomers after 1965. In fact, the term is not a legal designation and has no official definition, so in this book, we'll put "sanctuary city/state" in quotation marks.

Despite the national changes in tone embodied in the Hart-Celler Act and the Refugee Act of 1980, the reality is that many newcomers—both documented and undocumented—face a real threat of being returned to their countries of origin for any infraction and of being denied services by less knowledgeable or discriminatory providers in their new communi-ties. Refugees who left the system and immigrants who failed to become lawful permanent residents or were never documented in the first place are particularly at risk, especially if they come to the official attention of local police. Also, post-1965 presidents and congresses that have had differ-ing views of immigrants and refugees often encouraged stronger enforce-ment of immigration violations by federal officers, formerly referred to as Immigration & Nationalization Service (INS) and now called Immigration and Customs Enforcement (ICE).

As this conflict between national and local priorities grew, the "sanc-tuary city" movement gained momentum. Inspired by community polic-ing frameworks that proactively created connections between local police and different groups in a community, the fundamental statement of most "sanctuary cities" is that city officials will not go out of their way to assist federal officers in finding and apprehending undocumented persons, often with the caveat of "unless those persons run afoul of the law." They may make this proclamation in executive orders or public statements, or go as far as adopting legislation called TRUST Acts that lay out this policy. Police were an early focus because, as community policing gained traction, they found that crimes among newcomer communities often went unreported because the *victims*—not the criminals—feared deportation.

Most commonly, sources point to Special Order #40, issued by Los Angeles Chief of Police Daryl F. Gates, as the touchstone of the "sanctuary city" movement—a particularly interesting thing, because Gates was also known as a "law and order chief" who cracked down hard on local crime. In short, Special Order #40 1979 declared that LAPD officers may not initiate police action with the intent of discovering someone's immigration status, nor arrest them simply because they are undocumented. Further, only if a person is arrested for multiple misdemeanors or a single higher offense will they be officially listed as "undocumented" and potentially referred to federal agencies. The purpose of Special Order #40 was to reassure residents that "police services will be readily available to all persons, including the undocumented alien community, to ensure a safe and tranquil environment" (Gates 1979).

We don't know precisely when the term "sanctuary city" was first used, but it most likely came from earlier sanctuary movements: religious organizations would bring refugees to the United States and house them in their buildings, which do have official sanctuary status, as do consulates and embassies. It was certainly in use by 1987, when Governor of Massachusetts Michael Dukakis issued an executive order affirming the rights of equal access to services for all people living in the Commonwealth, regardless of citizenship or residency status. Shortly after this executive order, the aldermen of the city of Somerville issued their first Sanctuary City Resolution. These excerpts demonstrate the emotional weight of this document (Aldermen of Somerville 1989):

"WHEREAS, the United States has historically served as a haven for refugees of religious and political persecution . . .

WHEREAS, many persecuted people, particularly from Central America, Haiti, Brazil, and Ireland have come to Somerville where they have become productive members of our community . . .

WHEREAS, in response to this situation, some 350 religious communities across the nation, including one here in Somerville, have elected to provide sanctuary to refugees from Central America, in the belief that they are acting in accordance with international and federal law . . .

WHEREAS, 19 cities, including our neighbors in Cambridge and Brookline, and the state of Wisconsin have declared themselves as sanctuaries, cities and states of refuge for the oppressed . . .

WHEREAS, the city of Somerville has a diverse cultural heritage and multi-national population, of which the City is proud, and has historically welcomed newcomers . . .

(continued)

Therefore, be it RESOLVED, that the City of Somerville is hereby declared to be a City of Refuge and Sanctuary for oppressed people, particularly those from El Salvador, Guatemala, Haiti, Brazil, and Ireland and that they shall be afforded all rights and privileges offered and supplied to all people residing or working in the City . . .

and be it further RESOLVED, that the City of Somerville invites other United States cities, particularly our neighboring cities of Massachusetts, to join in the offer of sanctuary, so that the United States of America may serve as a friend to the suffering."

Buried in the list of WHEREAS's is one practical concern: "WHEREAS, the Board of Aldermen does not wish to expend City resources, beyond the requirements of federal law." In 2014, Mayor Joseph A. Curtatone of Somerville issued an executive order that spells that aspect out more specifically: "The Somerville Police Department has the discretion to honor an ICE detainer request. A request will be honored only if one or more of the following instances are met and if detaining the person would not violate any federal, state, or local law or policy." The rest of the order lists multiple criminal reasons why an ICE detainer request would be honored, and again specifies, "Somerville officials have a law enforcement or public safety purpose that is not related to the enforcement of civil immigration law" (Curtatone 2014).

Despite this long history, "sanctuary cities" fell off the national radar; they resurfaced quietly during the 2010s and returned with a vengeance after the 2016 presidential campaign. Presidential candidate Donald Trump was clear that, under his administration, "sanctuary cities" would be penalized by the withdrawal of federal aid monies. For many cities, federal aid contributes significantly to programs and services to residents, so the threat was potent.

In December 2016, after candidate Trump won the election, the current aldermen reaffirmed Somerville as a "sanctuary/TRUST Act city," specifying as a reason, "WHEREAS, while running for President, then-candidate Trump indicated that if he were elected, he would stop all Federal funding for Sanctuary Cities, also known as Trust Act Cities." The aldermen went on, "WHEREAS, Somerville has a strong and deep commitment to diversity and is proud of being a city that welcomes people from all around the world and is dedicated to ensuring that anyone living in Somerville, documented resident or not, can live in peace, safety, and be afforded protection from physical or emotional abuse, intimidation, or discrimination; NOW THEREFORE BE IT RESOLVED, That the Somerville Board of Aldermen goes on record reaffirming our commitment as a Sanctuary/Trust Act City . . . and BE IT FURTHER RESOLVED That no matter the threats made against sanctuary cities, Somerville will remain committed to our longtime policy and values and will not turn its back on the men and women from other countries who help make this city great" (Aldermen of Somerville 2016).

Catherine Piantigini, Deputy Director of the Somerville Public Library, relates, "The Mayor talked at length about Somerville being a sanctuary city [around the time of Trump's] inauguration in January. He's been very vocal about it in every piece of media" (Piantigini 2017). Indeed, over the first half of 2017, Mayor Curtatone took to Twitter to continuously reaffirm this stance both officially and personally. As of this writing, the city of Somerville website has a page dedicated to its history as a "sanctuary city": http://www.somervillema.gov/sanctuary.

How have libraries responded to the needs spelled out by the "sanctuary city" movement? David Leonard, president of the Boston Public Library, expressed it eloquently in a public statement made not long after Trump's inauguration: "Mayor Martin J. Walsh is resolute that Boston is and will remain a city of inclusion. The American Library Association and the Association of Research Libraries, to name two of the affiliations we hold close, have made affirming declarations of their commitments to equity, diversity, inclusion, and access. Boston Public Library and the 480+ staff members who serve our 26 locations are proud to stand with the Mayor and our library affiliates to reassert that we are *Free to All* and here to welcome everyone equally regardless of gender, race, national origin, sexual orientation, faith, or economic status . . . It is in times of uncertainty when we as an institution must reflect on and recommit to our founding principles—preserved in granite—that are the foundation from which every patron interaction originates" (Leonard 2017).

IMMIGRATION TERMS AND ACRONYMS

Throughout this book, you'll find many words and acronyms specific to the language of immigration. Let's take a moment to define them.

- **Newcomer/new arrival:** General-purpose term for anyone newly arrived to live in the United States.
- **New American:** "An all-encompassing term that includes foreign-born individuals (and their children and families) who seek to become fully integrated into their new community in the United States" (Muñoz & Rodriguez 2015).
- **Immigrant:** "An alien who has been granted the right by the USCIS to reside permanently in the United States and to work

without restrictions in the United States. Also known as a Lawful Permanent Resident (LPR)" (IRS n.d.).

- **Refugee:** "Generally, any person outside his or her country of nationality who is unable or unwilling to return to that country because of persecution or a well-founded fear of persecution based on the person's race, religion, nationality, membership in a particular social group, or political opinion" (USCIS n.d. C).

- **Lawful permanent resident (LPR):** "Any person not a citizen of the United States who is living in the U.S. under legally recognized and lawfully recorded permanent residence as an immigrant. Also known as 'permanent resident alien,' 'resident alien permit holder,' and 'Green Card holder'" (USCIS n.d. C).

- **Citizen:** "An individual born in the United States, Puerto Rico, Guam, or the U.S. Virgin Islands; whose parent is a U.S. citizen; or is a naturalized U.S. citizen" (IRS n.d.).

- **Undocumented:** "Anyone who has entered the United States illegally and is deportable if apprehended, or an alien who entered the United States legally but who has fallen 'out of status' and is deportable" (IRS n.d.).

- **Visa:** "A U.S. visa allows the bearer to apply for entry to the U.S. in a certain classification, such as student (F), visitor (B) or temporary worker (H). A visa does not grant the bearer the right to enter the United States" (USCIS n.d. C).

- **Naturalization:** "The process of applying for U.S. citizenship" (USCIS n.d. C).

- **U.S.-born:** Any resident born in the United States.

- **Receiving community:** "Any community—city, county, or state—where new Americans have made their homes. It includes longer-term residents, local governments, business leaders, educational institutions, faith communities, and others with a stake in building strong, united, and welcoming communities" (Muñoz & Rodriguez 2015).

- **Welcoming community:** "A community that strives to strengthen meaningful contact between immigrants and refugees and native-born residents, ensures inclusiveness, provides opportunity, and creates an overall positive environment for all" (Muñoz & Rodriguez 2015).

- **USCIS:** "U.S. Citizenship and Immigration Services, a federal agency in the Department of Homeland Security that oversees lawful immigration to the United States" (USCIS n.d. C).

- **ICE:** U.S. Immigration and Customs Enforcement, an agency of the Department of Homeland Security (USCIS n.d. C).

- **DACA:** Deferred Action for Childhood Arrivals, a program launched in 2012. Deferred means "an individual may remain in the United States for a set period of time, unless the deferred action is terminated for some reason; it's issued on a case-by-case basis and does not change immigration status by itself" (USCIS n.d. C).

BARRIERS TO IMMIGRANTS USING LIBRARIES

U.S.-born citizens have many reasons why they may not use a library: lack of awareness of current programs and services, incompatible hours or locations, or no sense of needing the library. Non–U.S.-born residents may have all of these reasons and others that are specific to newcomers:

Language barriers: If a new arrival is from a non–English-speaking country, a common language is usually the first barrier to library use. Even a newcomer with some English proficiency may not know the specific terms and phrases used in a library setting or be able to distinguish the cultural specifics of what they're looking for. Imagine asking for information about "the doors" and being directed to the music section rather than home repair, or vice versa when what you want is to know more about Jim Morrison's band.

Cultural barriers: Many newcomers are from countries without public libraries or places where libraries look and feel very different than they do in the United States. Newcomers may not just be unaware of what U.S. libraries offer, but what they fundamentally *are*. As a result, these newcomers don't seek out library services until someone mentions the library and what it can do; or when they are seeking a related service (such as voter registration or tax information) and are told "you can get that at the library." Cultural barriers may also include how present or absent women and children are in public life in a country of origin. This factor is changing as the awareness of gender equality increases globally, but for some cultures, women do not leave the house unaccompanied or interact often with people of the opposite sex outside the family. Understanding and being respectful of such cultural differences is an important part of reaching out to these community members.

Transportation barriers: Using public transportation and obtaining a driver's license can be difficult for those who do not speak English or didn't have a need for these things in their countries of origin. As for U.S.-born residents, the costs of private or public transportation to get to the library may be prohibitive, especially if newcomers are unemployed or underemployed.

Technological barriers: Although mobile devices have proliferated around the globe, they are not yet universal, especially for new-comers who are lower income or unemployed. Again, as with any-one in that situation, the increasing need for technological savvy to use library services—even the basics of accessing web-based email or renewing materials online—can be a challenge. Then there are the unintended consequences of steps like switching to "cashless" fine and fee payment; if someone cannot qualify for or does not have a credit card by choice, they are unable to use those conve-niences and need staff to help them work around the system.

Fear: In a Knight News Challenge grant application, the Buffalo and Erie County Public Library described the "fear-based barriers" that many newcomers feel regarding government agencies, includ-ing libraries. "A primary obstacle to engagement is mistrust and misunderstanding that the Library is a government state and hence dangerous. Some refugees and immigrants may believe that if they accept library services, even if for free, they will have to pay later or be denied citizenship. This will be addressed by meeting with their respected community leaders to educate that libraries have no law enforcement function. Library security officers will be outfitted with polo shirts, rather than uniforms, to remove any fear of being 'governmental or police-like.' Further, both libraries will create spaces where confidential interactions with relatives over-seas can occur via Skype" (Buffalo & Erie County Public Library 2016).

Undocumented persons: The perception of danger may, in fact, be very real for undocumented immigrants, who risk being discov-ered and potentially deported if they are in public spaces seeking services. The state of California is currently addressing this con-cern through Senate Bill (SB) #54, the California Values Act, which denotes certain public areas as "safe zones," in which someone can-not be detained simply on speculation about their immigrant sta-tus. We'll look again at SB54 in Chapter 7 on community building.

UNDOCUMENTED IMMIGRANTS

There are many reasons why a person may be an undocumented resi-dent of the United States. The media tends to focus on those who illegally cross borders by land or water, but the truth is often more mundane. In many cases, people remain here after their official travel or work visas expire, some intentionally, but others because they truly forgot to renew or thought they had and something happened to that application. Unfor-tunately, once you have overstayed your visa, you have nearly no recourse but to leave the country; for professionals or those who had residency through marriage and are now divorced, this can be a life-altering moment. They may have spent years legally building lives and careers in the United States and now, due to a moment of forgetfulness or a clerical error, must return to a country that may no longer be home.

Even more poignant are the stories of immigrants who have applied for Deferred Action for Childhood Arrival (DACA), sometimes referred to as DREAMers after an Obama administration program. Children, even teen-agers, often have no say in where their adult caregivers bring them. They did not necessarily choose to come to the United States in an undocu-mented way, but once here, they have the same barriers to gaining full citizenship as if they had made the choice themselves.

The topic of undocumented persons is frequently a sensitive one. Many of the library staff interviewed for this book noted that declaring that a service or program is explicitly for undocumented immigrants is not something that they can or will do, both for the library's protection and the immigrants' privacy. That said, everyone stated the need for libraries to serve all community members, regardless of immigration status.

Michelle Gordon, Community Librarian at the Fresno (CA) County Public Library, says, "It is incredibly important that libraries remain safe spaces for all community members. The Library does not care what coun-try you came from or what religion you practice or what shade your skin is. Our information is there for anyone who seeks it" (Gordon 2017).

Alicia Moguel, Principal Librarian and Associate Director of the Depart-ment of Lifelong Learning at the Los Angeles Public Library, expands on this idea: "We always welcome everybody. This is something the library does: we serve all people regardless of status. We don't require a Califor-nia DL [driver's license] to get a library card, we'll take any form of ID," no matter what country issued it, "and get them a library card . . . We know that here in LA, a lot of families are mixed status; you may have someone who is a citizen or lawful permanent resident, and they may have family members with them who are undocumented . . . We make it clear that we don't care where you come from, if you are here legally or not, whether you have status or not, we just want you to come in and use the library and the resources" (Moguel 2017).

Alicia's colleague, Madeleine (Maddy) Ildefonso, Senior Librarian in the Office of Enrichment and Empowerment, goes further: "[Undocumented persons have] integration issues because they have a lack of ability to nav-igate the system. They can't advance their rights as citizens, [though] as residents of the United States they do have constitutional rights. There's a lack of knowledge about those rights, and our job as a library is to help them become more informed, but that's our job with everyone" (Ildefonso 2017).

Los Angeles, in particular, and California, in general, are working steadily to increase the ability for both documented and undocumented immigrants to participate fully and legally in public life. The state of California offers a special driver's license to undocumented persons who can provide an identification document from a much broader list than a standard license requires; although these special licenses cannot be used as proof of identification, they do increase road safety by putting licensed and insured drivers behind the steering wheel. In Los Angeles, undocumented persons can vote for and sit on neighborhood councils and advisory boards under the city council, ensuring representation for and awareness of their communities.

INTEGRATION AND CELEBRATION

The programs and services described in this book address two needs felt by most newcomers to the United States: *integration* and *celebration*. Integration refers to how a new arrival becomes part of the fabric of their new community, and celebration highlights the unique aspects of a person's place of birth and their current home, no matter where they come from or live now.

The Networks for Integrating New Americans (NINA) project was an initiative led by World Education (http://www.worlded.org) that sought to identify and develop models for networks of partners to provide services to immigrants and new Americans. As part of NINA, immigrant integration was defined as "a dynamic, two-way process in which immigrants and the receiving society work together to build secure, vibrant, and cohesive communities" (Kallenbach & Nash 2016), based around three pillars identified by the White House Task Force on New Americans in 2015 (Muñoz & Rodriguez 2015):

- **Linguistic integration:** "When English learners have access to effective English language instruction to support their acquisition of English language skills, while also valuing and recognizing the importance of maintaining native language proficiency to preserve culture and intergenerational communication and expand economic opportunities."
- **Civic integration:** "When all community members belong, are secure in their rights and responsibilities, exercise their liberties, and share ownership in the community and our nation's future."
- **Economic integration:** "When both employers and immigrant workers understand their workplace rights and responsibilities,

and workers have resources to excel, embark on career pathways, and obtain economic self-sufficiency."

The NINA project developed a framework and model for collaborative impact in communities, supporting networks of partners led by a "back-bone organization" that coordinated the effort. Several libraries featured heavily in this book—Boise Public Library, Fresno County Public Library, and the libraries at the heart of the We Rhode Island network (WeRIN)—participated in the NINA project, often as backbone organizations.

The programs and services described in Chapters 2 through 6 fall under one or more of these pillars, from basic accessibility efforts to cultural cele-bration. Each topic will be explored in depth, illustrated by examples from libraries across the country.

2

◇ ◇ ◇

ACCESSIBLE LIBRARIES: IN-PERSON AND ONLINE

First impressions matter, whether it's a library user walking in the front doors or discovering a website in a search. If that first impression is positive, with friendly navigation that quickly leads the users to what they're looking for, it's more likely they will come back again. This is true regardless of where a user is from, but is especially true for newcomers, who may be more intimidated for all the reasons outlined in Chapter 1.

In this chapter, you'll examine the commitment needed to change to a more accessible library, including public declarations of support and mission and vision statements, then consider the possibilities of more accessible staff, physical building, basic services, and the library's web presence. Social media and beyond-the-building services are harder to control because you're working in someone else's space, but some of the same principles can be applied.

Two general principles emphasized in this chapter are:

- **Accessibility Helps Everyone:** Many of the suggestions in this book are inspired by the practices of usability and universal design. You'll look at these more closely later in the chapter.

- **American English:** Whenever language is discussed, it refers specifically to American English. It's important to remember that immigrants from British English–speaking countries or who learned English outside the United States are English speakers who might not be familiar with the American equivalents of the words they know. Similarly, conventions in mathematics and currency are different: I was once trying to help someone from Europe use an American calculator, and it was only when I remembered that some European countries use commas where the United States uses a decimal point—$1,00 rather than $1.00—that I could explain what was going on. (See http://www.statisticalconsultants .co.nz/blog/how-the-world-separates-its-decimals.html for more on this.)

Mary Jean Jakubowski, Director of the Buffalo and Erie County Public Library, offered her thoughts: "The best advice is to start small. Identify and meet with organizations in your area that are on the forefront of welcoming immigrants and refugees to the community. Identify one or two things that the library can do to support the transition process and work with these organizations [to implement them]. Simple steps like hanging welcome signage in native languages, ensuring staff is mindful and respectful of cultural customs, and meeting with members of your local immigrant and refugee community are all important components in making immigrants and refugees feel comfortable" (Jakubowski 2016).

COMMITMENT TO ACCESSIBILITY

While it's possible to implement change from the ground up, there's a far greater chance of systemic, lasting success if the support comes from the top. The stronger the message from municipal and library administration, the more likely that every member of the staff will see the importance of creating friendly, welcoming spaces for all residents, regardless of citizenship status. This support can be via public statements in response to specific events or more long-term commitments outlined in mission and vision statements.

Municipal Administrations

Because many public libraries are city, county, or other municipal agencies, the strongest signal of commitment to services to newcomers will come from the mayor's office or county seat. It can be a challenge to influence these governing bodies to support the library's agenda, but recent events have stirred the pot, leading many mayors and county governments to make statements of intent and support. At their 85th Annual Meeting in 2017, the U.S. Conference of Mayors issued a resolution, "Supporting Immigrants, Refugees, and Asylum Seekers and Standing Against Discriminatory and Harmful Policies That Target These Vulnerable Communities," calling on Congress to take actions against discriminatory policies and opposing "efforts to hold immigrants hostage as bargaining chips to threaten withholding federal funding from cities across the nation" (U.S. Conference on Mayors 2017).

Homa Naficy, Executive Director of the Hartford (CT) Public Library's The American Place, stresses this need for commitment at the top: "All of our leadership from the Mayor to the library director have been very supportive of this work . . . It's critical to any program to any population, having a leadership mind that is open to all, and recognizes the mission of the library as being open to all" (Naficy 2017).

For Mayor David H. Bieter of Boise, where refugee resettlements have been a state priority for 50 years, serving immigrants via the library is a political and personal priority—he's second-generation Basque American. Mike Journee, Director of Communication at the mayor's office, says, "The Mayor has made it a priority for all of us, across the 12 city departments, to reinforce the fact that we are a welcoming city. That we open our doors and our arms to people that are looking for refuge from some of the war-torn areas of the globe. The Mayor also recognizes that, other than city parks, the library is the one place that belongs to everyone. It is something that, no matter whether you are a child or a grandparent or an immigrant, no matter what, a library card can open up an entire world to these folks" (Journee 2017).

Moreover, says Journee, the mayor believes in the library of the future, not the past. "The idea of a 21st century library—the change in the way that libraries have approached their role, they're not just the racks and stacks any more. They are the place where people go to prepare themselves to become better, and I think that happens all across demographics" (Journee 2017). When Mayor Bieter took office in 2003, he was made aware that Boise's library service was among some of the worst in the country from a per capita basis. Along with his council members, he made it a priority to change that; Boise opened a fourth branch in May 2017 in a chronically underserved neighborhood largely inhabited by low-income residents and newcomers and is on the verge of a campaign to overhaul the Central Library.

Chapter 1 discussed the past and current position of Los Angeles city administrators on the issues around newcomers. Madeleine Ildefonso, of the Office of Enrichment and Empowerment, points to why it's vital that library staff know where the administration stands: "It's a consideration that any city employee thinks about, and that's why we work within the directives that are handed down from our city governance. We are in step with our higher authorities in the city, and so if someone complains, we are a bureaucratic hierarchical institution, the buck stops with the Mayor's office" (Ildefonso 2017). Alicia Moguel, Associate Director of the Department of Lifelong Learning, comes at it from the other direction: "We are basically supporting the work that our city government wants to happen in our city to serve its residents" (Moguel 2017). Either way, that alignment demonstrates the importance of these issues.

Library Public Statements

At the library level, declaring that services to newcomers is an organizational priority is a first step, followed by giving staff the support they need to fulfill that priority (which we'll look at in a moment).

If your mayor's office or county seat has issued a statement of support to newcomer populations, consider promoting it on the library's website or social media presence and state how the library provides services to newcomers, as they did at the Somerville Public Library. Deputy Director Catherine (Cathy) Piantigini expressed her thoughts on the mayor's position: "[After hearing Mayor Joseph Curtatone talk about Somerville being a Sanctuary City], I noticed that the Cambridge (MA) Public Library had done a nice piece about sanctuary cities and protecting immigrants and establishing the library as a place to go. I thought, 'We really need to do the same thing, to remind the city and the patrons what the library can do in times like these.' I worked with the reference department and the branches to make sure that all the resources we have for refugees and immigrants were up to date and that we had multiple copies of things available. We made [a resource list] available on the website and then posted it to Facebook and Twitter [along with a statement written by the head of reference] affirming . . . that we stood in line with the city and the mayor, and these are the things that we can do to support that" (Piantigini 2017). The Facebook post was one of the library's most successful, with more than 5,000 views.

In February 2017, a rally supporting the city's position was held at the neighboring high school and the library opened its doors. Cathy says, "The day before the rally at the high school, we would normally have closed at 6p but we stayed open until 8:30p. Beginning at 5p, we left the auditorium open with markers, tape, and posterboard, and people could gather and talk about the rally and make a sign if they wanted to. Residents, even if they're not directly involved with the services we offer, they're so pleased to know that the library is talking about it and that the city talks about it" (Piantigini 2017).

Chapter 1 quoted the first part of a public statement from David Leonard, president of the Boston Public Library, on the library's stance, and it continues with more specifics: "Boston Public Library and the 480+ staff members who serve our 26 locations are proud to stand with the Mayor. Our library services must remain available to all, without fear of discrimination . . . We work to help our users navigate the world. Whether they seek Boston Public Library services for intellectual growth, self-inquiry, academic support, or a multitude of other reasons, we serve as advocates for personal advancement and for clarifying the pathways to that achievement. And we will always protect our users' right to privacy in so doing. It is in times of uncertainty when we as an institution must reflect on and recommit to our found principles—preserved in granite—that are the foundation from which every patron interaction originates" (Leonard 2017).

When a library director issues a public statement that clearly describes the importance of continuing or improving services to immigrants, it sends a message to residents and to staff. If you feel a push to issue a statement, make sure it includes both the reasons why these services are important and, if possible, outlines what the library is currently and potentially going to do to serve local immigrant populations. This clarity can be a checklist for accountability: words alone aren't enough, but they are absolutely a starting point.

Mission and Vision Statements

Although these public statements are excellent short-term responses to current events, another place to indicate the library commitment to accessibility is in your mission or vision statement. If your library is in a strategic planning process and you haven't finalized your library mission or vision statement, add language to specify that newcomers to the community are especially welcome. If you have existing statements, explore the process to amend or update them before the next planning cycle. A few examples are shown here; pay special attention to the *italicized text*.

Language matters in these documents, but it doesn't need to be a battle ground. If you experience resistance to directly using words like "immigrant" or "refugee" in your statements, there are subtle ways to indicate these groups. The San José Public Library's Mission, Vision, and Values statement is a splendid example of this. Without ever using the words "immigrant" or "new American," they clearly include cultural and national diversity as things to be celebrated and supported.

In the mission statement, the library uses broad language to be inclusive: "San José Public Library enriches lives . . . by ensuring that *every member of the community* has access to a vast array of ideas and information" (San José Public Library n.d. D). In the vision statement, the word "cultural" becomes a catch-all for the many kinds of diversity—place of origin, race, religion, economic status, lifestyle, values, and more—represented in the city:

- "Library services that are known and valued by *the culturally diverse community . . .*"
- "A welcoming and lively *cultural* and lifelong learning center for the community."
- "A well-trained and highly capable *staff that reflects the diversity of San José . . .*"
- "*A close working relationship with other libraries, community agencies and organizations that foster cooperation . . .*" (This may refer, in part, to the community agencies and organizations that work with newcomers; we'll explore these potential partners in later chapters.) (San José Public Library n.d. D)

Finally, in the statement of values, the library makes their stance on who they serve and how: "Our users are not only our customers, they are the reason the library exists. *We provide quality service and treat all users fairly and equally. Services are provided in a non-judgmental manner that is sensitive to and supportive of human differences*" (San José Public Library n.d. D). This is a remarkable statement, and demonstrates the library's commitment to being a neutral, accessible space for everyone in the city of San José.

The city of New York directly addresses the needs of their immigrant populations through hundreds of targeted programs and services. This forthrightness is reflected in the mission and vision statements of the Queens (NY) Public Library, which include more direct language:

Mission: "The mission of the Queens Library is to . . . meet the informational, educational, cultural, and recreational *needs and interests of its diverse and changing population.*"

Vision: "As Queens Library enters its second century, it will be universally recognized as the most dynamic public library in the nation. *This recognition will arise from: the Library's dedication to the needs of its diverse communities; . . . We at Queens Library believe deeply in equity and that libraries are fundamental in empowering people to take charge of their lives, their governments and their communities.*"

Values: "**Customers**—*We believe that meeting the needs of our diverse customer base is first and foremost . . .*"; "**Individuality**—*We respect the individuality and integrity of each customer and each employee . . .*" (Queens Public Library n.d.)

Then, of course, there are unequivocal, clear statements like this 2017–2020 strategic goal from the Aurora (IL) Public Library: "**Welcome to America:** *New immigrants have information on citizenship, English language learning, employment, public schooling, health and safety, social services, and other topics they need to participate successfully in American life*" (Aurora Public Library n.d.).

Whatever ability you have to state clearly that your library is committed to being an open and welcoming place to immigrants and people from diverse cultures, use it to increase the staff and public awareness of that commitment.

ACCESSIBLE STAFF

One of the rallying cries of modern librarianship is that the attitude and abilities of staff are as or more important than the books on the shelves or computers in corners. Our buildings might be well-appointed and resource-heavy libraries, but without engaged and energetic staff, they can be cold and empty places. Creating a welcoming environment doesn't have to be an overwhelming undertaking; it can be as simple as a cheerful greeting and a willingness to listen and be patient.

Why the stress on staff attitudes? Because they make all the difference. Sophie Maier, Immigrant Services Librarian at the Louisville (KY) Free Public Library, talks about interactions she has with the large population of Muslim teenagers that frequent the Iroquois branch: "Since the election, I have a handful of kids who have had a lot of disciplinary trouble at school, but when they're here, they're able to express the fact that they're terrified. 'Am I going to be sent back? Why is my neighbor suddenly flying a Confederate flag? Should I walk the other way?' So that role of the public library is very important, steering them to a place where they can read news and get actual information on what to do if they're pulled over, to just listening and having that setting that's different than the school and what might be an antagonistic setting. They're acting out because they're terrified and freaking out, and I like that we're able to do that [be that place]" (Maier 2017).

In Norwalk, Connecticut, Moina Noor, library board member and unofficial liaison for her mosque, is certain that the librarians make the library what it is: "I really have to hand it to them, they really are such a warm and welcoming place for people who are new immigrants. A lot of our community's women cover their hair and they just feel very welcome there, and I think it has a lot to do with the people over there. I think that having the initial groundwork of making a place that feels so safe and comfortable for recent immigrants or people who may dress differently, I think that just lays a groundwork for trust later on." Noor stresses that staff diversity is a key element, "For non-white people or immigrant people, I think that if you just go in and there's just so many different kinds of people there already—it just kind of feeds on itself in a way" (Noor 2017).

Vicki Oatis, Director of Library Youth Services at the Norwalk Public Library, has a similar perspective: "Just by the nature of our community and what it is, we really have a great mix. When I look at the picture of the people who attended [a readers' theater program], so many cultures were represented and I just thought it was so indicative of our entire community. It made me think: how many other places in our community see that? . . . It's so representative of our community and I just feel very proud that that's what we have here at the library. I don't necessarily feel that we do anything but hopefully make people feel welcome" (Oatis 2017).

The next few sections will discuss ways to help increase the empathy and accessibility of your staff.

Staff Diversity

Obviously, one way to improve your library's reputation with immigrants and non-English speakers is to employ people from those communities at many levels of the library infrastructure. This isn't always easy, but having diverse representation among staff is undeniably beneficial to both library users and the performance of the library. I know of one library branch that essentially lost its Spanish-speaking customer base when the only native Spanish speaker on staff left for another location, and overall circulation dropped significantly due to those customers going elsewhere.

Improving staff diversity is a bigger topic than this brief section can address, but being open to the perspectives and skills of immigrant populations has to start at the top. Library administration needs to actively recruit from local communities, providing translated job descriptions for better understanding while also stressing that the job itself will require an appropriate level of English proficiency. Reach out to organizations that serve immigrant populations (see Chapter 7 on building community) and ask them to promote library job opportunities to their constituents. Library staff can also promote librarianship as a career path in newcomer communities to help diversify students entering library school. The benefits of creating a diverse staff have an impact not only on your users, but on staff themselves. Homa Naficy of Hartford described it succinctly: "Fortunately, our library and our branches are very diverse. Nobody feels 'different'—you very much feel like a part of something bigger" (Naficy 2017).

As the importance of a diverse workplace has become clearer over the past few years, many studies and reports have offered more specific strategies for increasing that diversity. A few that apply specifically to libraries include:

Build partnerships with communities of color and other underrepresented groups. Although the focus of this book—especially Chapter 7—is about building partnerships within and around immigrant communities, connecting to and promoting library employment within local communities of U.S.-born people of color is just as important. Other groups to focus diversity efforts on are people with disabilities, people re-entering the workforce after incarceration, "second-career" applicants, and LGBTQQ+-identified persons.

Create an inclusive environment that shows all staff are valued. Ensure that staff in all roles at the library feel their voices, experiences, skills, and interests are valued. This feeds into the "feeling a part of something bigger" that Homa mentioned. Create tools for sharing feedback and skills/interests, and make sure all staff feel they have equal access to them; the emotional aspect of that access is as important as getting a login or being able to slip a piece of paper into a box.

Develop goals for increasing staff diversity. These are different from affirmative action or other legal requirements; they are specific to your organization and should be both measurable and reasonably achievable given current resources.

Broaden the applicant pool, especially for higher-level positions. Seek out the broadest possible applicant pool for library-degree required and management/supervisory positions. Re-evaluate critical qualifications and determine other ways for applicants to meet those requirements. Work with large organizations like the Black Caucus of the American Library Association (www.bcala.org) to promote positions nationally.

Create opportunities for and support young staff of underrepresented groups. Create mentorship opportunities and build support networks for staff as they scale the library hierarchy. Consider creating "individual contributor" positions for those who want to advance their career but prefer not to go into management (NGen Fellows 2014).

The ALA Office for Diversity, Literacy, and Outreach Services has links to many additional resources at http://www.ala.org/aboutala/offices /diversity.

Language Learning and Translation

As you work to increase the overall diversity among staff, there are steps to take that help U.S.-born staff better serve newcomers. An ultimate goal for newcomers is to learn English to ease their transition to life in the United States, but a little accommodation by staff goes a long way toward building the sense of trust that Moina mentioned and can be a part of that education.

When hiring, stress the need for native English speakers who are also fluent in other languages; offer hiring bonuses or higher starting pay grades, if possible, to entice qualified applicants. For current staff, encourage them to increase their proficiency in community-relevant languages. Many people pick up a few of the most important transactional words just by interacting with customers, but many staff would benefit from the structured learning experience of a workshop or class. For in-service staff training, work with local immigrant community members or organizations to develop "Top 10 Library Terms & Phrases" workshops in each target language. Make these language trainings part of meetings and all-staff training days. There are many possibilities, but start with terms like:

- Directions (left, right, upstairs, downstairs), escalator, stairs, door, floor (of a building)
- Bathrooms, parking lot, community room
- Book (other formats tend to use the English term)
- Information needed to get a library card: given name, family name, address, phone number, email address
- Circulation terms: check out, return, renew, fee/fine, and the phrase "pay your fee/fine"
- Numbers, dates, and currency
- Library program phrases: story time or stories for children, film, craft, lecture

Use the same process to develop cheat sheets to keep at service points, ideally with the phrase in English, the transliterated language, and the original script if applicable. Look at "point-to-the-word" books and cards designed for travelers for more ideas on how to assemble cheat sheets in multiple languages.

If staff are interested in more comprehensive language training, take the next step and offer them the time and—if possible—funding needed to attend language workshops or classes. Truly self-directed staff can use off-desk time to work through an online/app-based learning program like Duolingo or whichever language learning platform your library subscribes to. Community colleges and centers for adult education can be less expensive places for multiweek in-person classes, and there are many options for instructor-led online language learning. If enough staff are interested, consider hiring a language instructor for onsite training, which has the advantage of providing tailored content for your staff and more bang for your training dollars.

If staff themselves aren't fluent in other languages and you have an immediate need, consider on-the-spot translation services. The Madison (WI) Public Library offers phone-based translation services for users; staff have the number handy at all times to simply call and work through the translator to help their patron. At the Boise Public Library, this service is citywide and coordinated by city offices, says Sarah Kelley-Chase, branch supervisor at the Bown Crossing location. "If staff get into a situation where we can't find anyone to interpret, we can call these numbers and have an intermediary translate for us. I haven't had an opportunity to use it yet but it's nice to know that it's available" (Kelley-Chase 2017).

Go Mobile!

With the move toward mobile in-library assistance, web-based translations via a tablet in the stacks become possible and perhaps even more helpful than a phone, because you can work with the materials directly. Although not perfect, a service like Google Translate might still be useful in a pinch.

If you have a particular program that you'd like to make sure is accessible to non-English speakers, considering having a translator on hand for the event. When Vicki Oatis ran a Harry Potter–themed escape room at the Norwalk Public Library, she remembered the many Spanish speakers in her community. "You don't want to not include people," she says, and although many of the clues didn't require English, having a Spanish speaker on hand could be helpful for questions. "Initially, I thought maybe we could have times that if Spanish speakers wanted to come in. But one of our key creators of the escape room was Library Assistant Urania Avery (her family is from Colombia), who is extraordinarily creative, and I cannot tell you how lucky I am to have her here—she does all the displays and stuff that I can't do. She was going to be there and I asked her, if families come who we know primarily speak Spanish, could you make sure you're here and in the room to be here to help translate? I thought that would work better than having specific Spanish times because it's much more limiting that way. We had one group that did need some translation—they came as a family—and it was helpful to have her there" (Oatis 2017).

To summarize ways to reduce the patron/staff language barriers at your library:

- Hire multilingual staff, either from newcomer communities or among U.S.-born hires.
- Provide library-specific language training as staff development.
- Offer staff support to take online or in-person classes to improve fluency.
- Create "cheat sheets" of useful phrases to keep at service points.
- Provide translation by phone or mobile device.
- Have translators available at key programs and events.
- Offer library marketing and informational material in other languages (Chapter 7 will address this topic in more detail).

Cultural Awareness

Part of good customer service is understanding how to interact respectfully and effectively with patrons, and understanding the social norms of other cultures can be a huge help. For instance, in more observant denominations of Islam and Judaism, men and women do not casually touch except between family members; knowing this fact means not being offended if someone of the opposite gender from those traditions will not shake your hand. There's no insult meant; it's simply not in their culture to do so. In the same way, when staff know the names of and differences between the many male and female head coverings found throughout Asia and Africa, they demonstrate respect and interest for those cultures, which helps foster trust and warmth between the library and its community.

- Sikh men and women: dastaar, turban, pagri/pagg
- Muslim women: abaya, burqua, chador, cowl, ghoonghat, niquab, paranja (Uzbek), tagelmust (Tuareg), tudung (Malay)

Like language trainings, cultural awareness can come via many different modes. If your library hosts cultural showcases or sharing programs (discussed in Chapter 6), encourage staff to attend and arrange the desk coverage to let as many staff as possible do so. Invite members of the community to speak at staff meetings and possibly answer questions, including the awkward questions staff might not feel comfortable asking patrons while on the service floor.

As you develop your collections to include and respond to the changing cultures in your community, encourage staff to use those resources to learn more themselves. Use nonfiction series for children on world cultures as the basis for staff "winter reading lists" (or whenever is your slowest season). Watch documentaries about different immigrant groups during staff meetings or in-service days. Throughout this informal learning, encourage staff to share their insights on how what they see or read compares with the lived reality of immigrants in your area.

There are also many books and online resources about different countries designed for people doing business or other negotiations in those places. One title to find is *Kiss, Bow, or Shake Hands: The Bestselling Guide to Doing Business in More Than 60 Countries, 2nd Edition* by Terri Morrison, a book from 2006 that is still recommended in multinational companies.

Finally, as with language, you could directly provide staff training on the cultures represented in your community, either through brief information sessions or more involved workshops. Partners from organizations serving newcomer communities are good places to find instructors, or check out local cultural organizations. If your local college or university has an international business or government policy program, professors or graduate students there can be fantastic sources for trainings and advice.

A hands-on list of ways to encourage staff to increase their awareness and understanding of local newcomer cultures:

- Support staff to attend cultural programs at the library.
- Encourage staff to attend open houses or welcoming events at local cultural or religious organizations. (Chapter 7 contains a spectacular example of what can come from these visits.)
- Invite members of newcomer communities who are willing to come to staff meetings to discuss their culture and answer questions.

- Ask staff to learn about and share information about local immigrant populations.
- Provide cultural awareness training, but make sure to avoid dated language like "sensitivity training."

ACCESSIBLE BUILDINGS

Building on a foundation of warm and welcoming staff, consider what you can do with your physical space to make it more inviting and easier to use for people who may not have any idea of what a public library is or what they can find there, or who have low English literacy skills.

- Signage/wayfinding, including consideration of cultural norms
- Collections
- Community information

First, consider the basic principles of usability and universal design, principles that can be applied to buildings, signage, documents, and websites. Usability describes the quality of a user's experience when interacting with products or systems, physically and online. You can evaluate whether something is easily useable by looking at how intuitive it is, whether a person needs extensive instruction to use it, how efficient it is and how many errors someone makes, how easy it is to remember how to use the thing the next time, and how much a person enjoys using it. Visit Usability.gov or any of the resources mentioned at the end of the section on accessible websites for more information.

Universal design, in contrast, starts with an idea or existing product or system and tests to see how easy it is for *all* users to work with, based on its equitability, flexibility, intuitiveness, tolerance for error, and physical accessibility. Its principles were developed as part of making buildings, objects, and systems more accessible to persons with disabilities, but they can be applied by focusing on unfamiliarity with the language and culture of the United States as a reason for challenges rather than a disability. For more on universal design, visit the Center for Universal Design at http://projects.ncsu.edu/ncsu/design/cud/.

Signage and Wayfinding

Today's libraries are complex enough that the old floor plan—circulation, adult fiction, adult nonfiction, reference, children's room—has been replaced by many distinct areas. As libraries have added services (audio-visual collections, public computers, teen/tween spaces, literacy/multilanguage collections, and more), wayfinding inside the building has become imperative. A reasonable amount of signage in appropriate languages can help anyone find where they want to go, though we'll look at the perils of oversignage in a moment.

Large, legible area signs are a must, and it's better to use language that people new to both the United States and American English can understand. "Circulation" or "Reference" might be unfamiliar, but "Checkout" and "Information" or "Research" are terms they see everywhere. Many studies have shown that even native English speakers who use libraries have trouble understanding library jargon; improve everyone's user experience by featuring the words they use, not ones you require them to learn to understand your services.

Translating signs can be a slippery slope, because how many languages should or could you translate them into? Sometimes, it's as straightforward as English and Spanish, but many communities now have 10, 20, 30, or many more languages represented—several libraries in this book mentioned upwards of 100 languages in their area. Sophie Maier of Louisville reports, "We have 136 different languages spoken in our school system, and a lot of them are in my branch's neighborhood" (Maier 2017). If you can narrow the field down to five or fewer high-impact languages, consider translating high-priority signs (especially los baños). If there are too many, keep your signage in English and provide staff with cheat sheets of important phrases (see more on this in the earlier section on staff language learning). If your library is moving to mobile-supported roving reference, make sure an international travel language app or translator app is loaded on staff mobile devices.

One place where signage in languages other than English would be useful is among collections of materials in those languages. If your collections are large enough to warrant it, add the same sort of internal subject or format descriptions as you display in the corresponding English-language sections. If you know that Russian romance novels circulate like hotcakes, mark their shelves with любовные романы so Russian readers can find them quickly.

In all cases, for accurate translations, ask a staff or community member to translate, or use a professional translation service. *Do not rely on web-based translation services.* Many of the terms and phrases needed for library signage are idiomatic and will suffer badly from the direct, word-by-word approach of machine translation. It's best to work with someone who speaks the specific dialects in your area, but a formal-sounding translation is still better than what a machine can produce. (For amusing and

occasionally offensive examples of bad translations, visit www.engrish
.com.)

Be careful about simply changing from text to icons; icons and images
are their own language and can mean different things to different people.
Icons also rarely age gracefully: Does anyone still use floppy disks to save
on, or cassettes to record audio on? If you want to really cover your bases,
use a combination of single words and a simple icon for large signs—
"Information" with an "i" inside a circle—and teach your users your icon
language as they navigate around the building. Then, you can use just the
icon in places where you need something smaller and your users will
understand.

Similarly, color coding can be helpful, but do a little research on the cultural significance of colors to the immigrant groups in your community
before you take them too far. White in American culture is peace and
"goodness," but in some Asian cultures it's the color of death; red tends
to mean anger, danger, or sex in the United States, but is the color of good
luck and happiness in China. Get feedback from foreign-born residents of
the community before committing to color schemes that mean more or
other than you intend them to.

For more on library signage:

- ALA TechSource presentation: http://www.slideshare.net/ALA
  TechSource/effective-library-signage-tips-tricks-and-best
  -practices
- Best Practices for Customer-Focused Library Design: http://www
  .webjunction.org/content/dam/WebJunction/Documents
  /webJunction/CFLBestPractices.pdf
- Wayfinding the San José Way, a blog series and webinar hosted by
  Demco on how San José Public Library redesigned its physical
  library experience. The blog series starts with http://ideas.demco
  .com/blog/library-signs/ and the webinar is at http://ideas.demco
  .com/webinar/wayfinding-san-jose-way

Collections

These days, finding materials in the most common non-English European languages—Spanish, Portuguese, French, German—is relatively
straightforward. Spanish materials in particular are a part of most library
distributors' catalogs, and there are multiple Spanish-language publishers
in the United States and other parts of the world. It's even possible to find

materials that are written in Latin American Spanish or a country-specific dialect of it, rather than European Spanish. Work with your primary suppliers to find out what languages they can help you collect, and tell them what languages you need to help them guide their research efforts into new areas. Remember that for several countries, immigrants may be fluent and literate in both a European language and other local languages, such as Haitian immigrants knowing French and Haitian Kreyol/Creole, and may look for materials in both or prefer one to the other.

For other languages, finding materials is still difficult, bordering on impossible, especially for original-language books and videos as opposed to translations of English works. However, before you knock yourself out looking for these items, *make sure your immigrant patrons want or need them.* For a wide variety of reasons, it may not be necessary to collect materials in some languages, including the possibility that a language may not have a written form or that the populations of that language's speakers in your area aren't able to read it. Develop relationships with new immigrant populations first, invite them into your programs and English-based services, then begin to find out whether and what reading or viewing material might interest them.

When the Boise Public Library was planning its new Bown Crossing location, says Sarah Kelley-Chase, "we didn't open with tons and tons of materials in different languages because we wanted to wait to see how it shook out as far as what kinds of requests we were getting. We had a lot of children's materials, especially in Spanish, but we're starting to get adult materials in Somali, Arabic, Farsi. Our collection development team is working really hard to try and find places to source materials, especially more authentic literature, not just something written in English and translated into a language but something written in the original language" (Kelley-Chase 2017).

Homa Naficy sees the same issue in Hartford: "Hartford isn't one of the wealthier cities in the nation—it's one of the poorer—and the immigrant population that we're working with is struggling, for the most part. Some come with a decent educational background . . . but for the most part their education is low and they're from agrarian backgrounds. That changes their basic needs. The biggest needs that would bring them into the library are English language classes and anything that has to do with immigration . . . then [they're looking for a] computer where they can access radio and information from their old country and, for the more literate, they can access newspapers from their old country. We do have collections in Spanish; that's our primary language, and our second largest population is

West Indian, who speak English. In the less visible languages, we have refugees that are resettled, but for the most part their literacy in their native language is low to zero. Providing that material is not very helpful—for instance, the Bantu language didn't even have a written script until the late 1970s" (Naficy 2017).

If you choose to collect in multiple languages, the problem is often finding a steady supply of new materials. Many of the librarians I spoke with say that this is as much a challenge in the globalized 21st century as it was a few decades ago. Again, the best suggestion is to focus your efforts, as the collection development librarians of Boise have in their current foreign language plan. Kathleen Stalder, Acquisitions and Technical Services Assistant Supervisor for Collection Development, says, "We've realized that we aren't able to provide a quality collection when we are trying to collect for all possible languages. We discussed at length how much time, money, and space we dedicate to English language materials, and we still aren't able to meet every need within our community. Once we recognized that, it drove home the point that we needed to change our approach to providing materials in other languages and really focus our resources where they would have the most impact" (Stalder 2017).

Depending on your resources and budget, any of the following might be paths to finding the hottest new novel or quality nonfiction:

Ask for help: If you ask your new patrons whether they want these materials, also ask if they have any favorite titles or publishers to recommend. If you see people with materials in those languages, ask them for help in finding the publisher name and contact information, if possible.

Ask for donations: Encourage avid readers among your immigrant patrons to donate their books to the library.

Check out cultural grocery stores and markets: Just as with mainstream supermarkets, small "ethnic" markets often have books and videos on sale. Purchase directly from the store, or ask the owner where they get their supplies from and see if that company will work with you. Develop a relationship with the store owner and work together to increase your reach; the proprietor might be willing to donate overstock materials to the library, especially in exchange for having a flyer on your community information board.

Try Amazon: Especially if you have native speakers on staff or have made connections in the community, see if there's a country-specific Amazon store and try ordering online. You're not purchasing for resale, but make sure that you don't run afoul of local copyright laws. If nothing else, you can use Amazon to put together a purchase list and then try more traditional methods of acquiring the materials.

Keep searching online for distributors of materials in a specific language: Every few months, run the search again and see if something new has come up. Kathleen at Boise says they've had good luck with Sawa Books (http://sawabooks.com). "The materials are very well put together, and each item comes with a cataloging aid—our cataloger loves them!" (Stalder 2017).

Visit the country: If someone on staff or a well-known patron is going to that country—either to visit relatives or as travel—ask them to bring back a few popular titles and/or take note of publishers.

Consider local authors: As you develop relationships, find out if there are any budding authors or, possibly more immediately useful, people who want to tell their own stories and self-publish. Add some of these materials, but be aware of quality control issues.

Community Information

From bulletin boards to binders, local information is a vital piece of what makes a library a community hub. By extending your community information materials to include resources explicitly for immigrants and refugees, or information in all the languages it's available in, you can increase their accessibility.

When you're considering sources of material, be inspired by but not limited to the following. In particular, many states and cities have driver's education and health information available in multiple languages that you can get by directly contacting the offices and asking for them. Avoid creating visual clutter by focusing on high-impact languages and information that promotes an entire program or service rather than individual events.

- Citizenship offices
- City/county immigration affairs departments
- Community- and faith-based organizations for specific immigrant groups
- For-fee English language classes for newcomers who want more than the library's free offerings
- Legal aid resources, both national networks and local resources

- Driver's education materials
- Affordable housing and food assistance resources
- Health provision and insurance information
- Grassroots initiatives to help low-income or struggling families

Community information can also come in the form of events and services. As part of a comprehensive "Community Welcomes You" project (a semifinalist in the 2016 Knight News Challenge), the Buffalo & Erie County Library developed the idea of "Welcome Days": an opportunity for new residents to meet representatives of community organizations and city agencies to learn more about essential services, including education, housing, healthcare, transportation, employment, and citizenship. "[Welcome Days] can connect these residents with services that could benefit their families, helping to make an easier transition into the community. . . . By providing an onsite aid, as well as materials and easy online library website navigation, the library can better serve a local growing, underserved population" (Buffalo and Erie County Public Library 2016). Although the library designed these Welcome Days for newcomers, they also sound like a fantastic opportunity for all new residents of the area to learn more about their community services, regardless of where they're from.

In Hartford, Connecticut, the library's immigrant services program is called The American Place and includes citizenship aid, English-language learning, job assistance, and community information. The American Place also coordinates the library's Cultural Navigator program, a volunteer effort to provide cultural mentors to new immigrants as they adjust to living in Hartford. By working with individuals or families at least two hours a week for a three-month period, Cultural Navigators help reduce the stress of cultural adjustment by introducing new arrivals to city and library services, helping them practice English, and explaining cultural differences in their new community.

Initial meetings happen at the library so mentors can orient newcomers to the library, including The American Place, and be lightly monitored by library staff, especially if the newcomer family includes children. Through in-person and online trainings from the library, Cultural Navigators practice listening with care and interest, learn more about city and state services, and learn how to fill out necessary reports. The program also includes special group events and activities run by the library; bus tokens are available to mentors after the first 21 hours of meetings if they want to accompany their family to visit other public service locations.

ACCESSIBLE SERVICES

Many services at libraries are, by default, as equally useful or interesting to newcomer users as lifelong residents: public technology, computer classes, story times, news sources, language learning, driver's education materials, community information, health information, research materials. Now that you've learned ways to improve your collections and community information, consider accessibility. (Note: Career and job assistance are covered in Chapter 5 and cultural programs are discussed in Chapter 6.)

Beyond multilingual programs and/or translators, the fundamental way to make the essential services mentioned earlier accessible to newcomers is to talk about them—often. Whether someone is brand new in this country or has been here for decades, no matter what their proficiency level in English, the dedication to providing those services that were talked about at the beginning of this chapter comes most to the fore by making newcomers feel welcomed in all programs and to use all services at the library. After you've invited them to use English-language programs or materials, they might decide that they need something in their own language or would prefer a translator and will feel confident enough about your willingness to help that they'll ask for them.

Vicki from Norwalk mentions that although targeted programs are good, many folks are looking for English programs to practice listening to and speaking the language. "We have so many parents come in and tell us that they're looking for the fact that most of our story times are in English. We have a large Polish population and that's how the kids are learning English, is by coming to the story times" (Oatis 2017). Sarah in Boise makes the same point: "The services that we have for everyone can also be used for services to immigrants. Scanners for people to scan their documents can be used to get documents for citizenship, computers to help people find news in their languages or from their home countries, or emailing to send for citizenship or communicate with family members who are still back in their home country. Most often it's a situation where they need to scan their ID or other documents for working towards citizenship or for bringing someone else over, and then send them by email" (Kelley-Chase 2017).

That said, you can add elements to your essential services that are specifically useful to immigrants and refugees. At the Buffalo & Erie County Public Library, they've installed Skype on dedicated public computers for immigrants and refugees to use to communicate with their families back home; the software itself doesn't cost anything, and individuals can log in with their own accounts. The library has also added SCOLA—original resources in more than 175 native languages, including TV program-ming from around the world—to their database collection. On your pub-lic computers, make sure that the ability to switch languages is enabled and updated, if needed. Ask your technology and resource vendors what materials are available in languages other than English or are geared for an international audience and determine if they're worth the cost.

For library events, consider programs that either remove the need for instruction in English—Chapter 6 describes a coloring program that was surprisingly popular with a diverse audience—or provide translation as discussed earlier. Again, many participants may want the English-language programs for practice, but may also appreciate situations where their language skills aren't as necessary or their multilingualism is an asset.

Enhanced Content

If you're running a program like an escape room, create a situation where you *can* solve it with an all–English-speaking group, but added content opens up if you have people who speak other languages, pulling from the primary languages spoken in the area. For instance, have a clue that's in English but includes a phrase in Vietnamese or Thai that says, "There's another treasure down the hall."

ACCESSIBLE WEBSITES

As with the physical building, the principles of usability and universal design apply to your library website, improving services to all of your users while assisting non-native English speakers in particular. Improving overall usability can be a significant commitment of time and resources, but a streamlined, easily usable site will require less effort to translate, and so let's look at that first.

Usability Improvements

In website design, *usability* refers to making the content and navigation of the site as intuitive and readable as possible; site *accessibility* for low vision or other needs refers to how easy it is for screen readers and other assistive devices to work with. By streamlining your content text, improving your site structure and navigation, and including image alt text, you make it easier for anyone to find information on your site.

Fewer, Plainer Words

Simplifying language on your website is the most straightforward thing you can do to reduce the online language barrier. Simple language isn't dumbed down or casual, just stripped of extras that make comprehension more difficult for visitors with lower English literacy. For a quick evaluation of your site content, try a readability test like Read-able (http://www .webpagefx.com/tools/read-able): visit their site, paste a page URL from your site into the box, and hit Enter. You'll get an overview score at the top and scores on specific rating scales (red for less readable, green for more readable) down below.

The best method for simplifying site content is to review the site section by section and create a content list, prioritizing the pages for their relevance to the majority of your users (not by how important you think they are to your users). Next, in priority order, review the text on each page and edit until it's as simple and densely informative as possible, without becoming uselessly vague. Finally, after removing words, rewrite what's left using simple declarative language. PlainLanguage.gov is a resource created in 2010 by an initiative to simplify the language of federal websites, including the IRS's. It explains what constitutes plain language and offers tips on revising your site text to meet those criteria (PlainLanguage.gov n.d.).

Document Checklist for Plain Language

- Written for the average reader
- Organized to serve the reader's needs
- Has useful headings
- Uses "you" and other pronouns to speak to the reader
- Uses active voice
- Uses short sections and sentences
- Uses the simplest tense possible—simple present is best
- Uses base verbs, not nominalizations (hidden verbs)
- Omits excess words
- Uses concrete, familiar words
- Uses "must" to express requirements; avoids the ambiguous word "shall"
- Places words carefully (avoids large gaps between the subject, the verb, and the object; puts exceptions last; places modifiers correctly)
- Uses lists and tables to simplify complex material
- Uses no more than two or three subordinate levels

SOURCE: https://plainlanguage.gov/resources/checklists/checklist/

(continued)

Document Checklist for Plain Language on the Web

On the web, people are in a hurry. They skim and scan, looking for quick answers to their questions. Help your readers quickly find what they need with these web writing tips:

- Less is more! Be concise.
- Break documents into separate topics.
- Use even shorter paragraphs than on paper.
- Use short lists and bullets to organize information.
- Use even more lists than on paper.
- Use even more headings with less under each heading.
- Questions often make great headings.
- Present each topic or point separately, and use descriptive section headings.
- Keep the information on each page to no more than two levels.
- Make liberal use of white space so pages are easy to scan.
- Write (especially page titles) using the same words your readers would use when doing a web search for the info.
- Don't assume your readers have knowledge of the subject or have read related pages on your site. Clearly explain things so each page can stand on its own.
- Never use "click here" as a link—link language should describe what your reader will get if they click the link.
- Eliminate unnecessary words.

SOURCE: https://plainlanguage.gov/resources/checklists/web-checklist/

Improve Site Navigation

After streamlining your content, simplifying your site structure and navigation is a natural second step to improving site usability. This requires effort on the part of your site administrator(s), but will make your website a powerful tool for all users.

Good site navigation is clear, obvious, and self-guided. Users always know where they are on the site and can make reasonable guesses on where to find what they're looking for. Unnecessary or duplicate pages are removed, and the remaining pages are grouped into as few sections as is useful. Visually, this means that each page is uncluttered, with additional information one obvious click away. Site menus are easy to find and use multiple methods to point users toward the next page. Pages are broken into section headings, which can be linked to from within the page and listed at the top of a longer page when absolutely necessary.

Most content management systems (CMSs) support creating menus and site architecture, and changing these structures can be as simple as choosing new parent or child pages and/or dragging and dropping page names into a menu list. If your site is built on static HTML files, changing the architecture and menus is much more complex and requires extensive coding knowledge. As a suggestion, if you were considering switching from static HTML to a content management system anyway, this project might be a good opportunity to seek outside funding targeted for "improving the library website for the use of immigrants." It would do so, and at the same time, improve the library website for everyone else.

Add Metadata and Descriptions

While you're improving linguistic accessibility—especially if you end up redesigning your entire site—now is a fantastic time to add general accessibility elements, such as alt text descriptions and code that interacts well with assistive technologies. It's beyond the scope of this book to talk much about these here, but there are many library-focused resources on creating more accessible websites:

- ARL Web Accessibility Toolkit: http://accessibility.arl.org/external-resources
- WebAIM (Web Accessibility In Mind): http://webaim.org/articles
- W3C Web Accessibility Initiative (WAI): http://www.w3.org/WAI
- ASCLA Tip Sheets on Accessibility: http://www.ala.org/ascla/resources/tipsheets

This is only a brief overview of improving site usability. My personal web usability library includes these and many more titles. These resources are listed according to their relevance and appeal to a nongeeky audience; if you only get two, get King's and Redish's books.

- *Designing the Digital Experience* by David Lee King, Digital Branch & Services Manager at the Topeka and Shawnee County (KS) Public Library.
- *Letting Go of the Words: Writing Web Content that Works*, 2nd ed. by Janice (Ginny) Redish. This is still the single best book I've found on writing quality web content for any online service.
- *Don't Make Me Think: A Common Sense Approach to Web Usability*, 3rd ed. by Steve Krug. Updated for a content management and mobile app century.
- *The User Is Always Right: A Practical Guide to Creating and Using Personas for the Web* by Steve Mulder with Ziv Yaar. Again, a single best resource on developing a better sense of who your users are

and how they might and do use your services. Not just good for websites, you can create personas for in-person services and physical spaces, too.

- *Forms that Work: Designing Web Forms for Usability* by Caroline Jarrett and Gerry Gaffney. Does for web forms what *Letting Go of the Words* does for content.

Additional web-based resources on usability:

- PlainLanguage.gov—http://www.plainlanguage.gov
- Usability.gov—http://www.usability.gov
- Janice Redish's site, specifically the articles and slides: http://www.redish.net/articles-a-slides
- Steve Krug's site Advanced Common Sense: http://sensible.com/index.html

Translation

After you've given your site content a usability trim, translating some or all of your content into relevant languages will make it more accessible for those with very limited English. As with signage, using a machine translation tool like Google Translate is inexpensive and easier to implement, but can result in less accurate translations. Human translation can be more expensive, but you will get what you pay for. Definitely explore both options rather than simply choosing one; custom translation of a few key pages may be more cost effective and useful in the long run than semiaccurate machine translations on all of them.

Google Translate

One of the most ubiquitous translation tools out there, a Google Translate drop-down menu is in the upper-right corner of millions of web pages. This is partly because Google makes it simple to generate the code: you visit http://translate.google.com/manager/website/?hl=en, choose your options, and copy and paste their generated code onto each page of your site that you want translated. Alternatively, if you have the site maintenance skills or are using a content management system, you can place the code where it will be globally added to every page on your site.

Although simple, using Google Translate runs the risk of inaccurate translations that are, at best, amusing and, at worst, hopelessly useless. However, it is said that the perfect is the enemy of the good, and if your goal is to increase your accessibility quickly and easily, Google Translate is a tool for that.

Content-Driven Translation

Manually translating your website requires a larger investment of time and/or money, but results in controlling precisely what gets translated and what the quality of that translation is.

In 2014, the Multnomah (CO) County Library made the decision to focus on improving services to different language groups through hiring multilingual staff, providing multicultural programming, and translating the library's website. Jeremy Graybill, Marketing + Online Engagement Director, describes the process: "The library focused on the most prominent languages in our area: Spanish, Russian, Chinese and Vietnamese. Making the website available in these languages was really a no-brainer: it was not only a usability/equity issue, it was demonstrating our commitment. Recently our language efforts have expanded to include some Somali as well, but not on the website" (Graybill 2017).

After evaluating Google Translate, which they described as "the quality of translations is poor and overlaying the Google Translate functionality completely negated the mobile-responsiveness of the site, so that was a deal breaker," Multnomah chose to go with human translation and manually add it to their content management system, Drupal. They used a local professional translation service at a price of $0.22 per word (another reason to do your usability content work first), and translating all appropriate content into four languages cost approximately $24,000. Additional content is translated or updated as needed, and maintenance costs are around $2,000 per year. Their mobile app is also available in five languages and utilizes the same translated content.

The Drupal content management system supports two modes of site translation: entity translation and content translation. Without getting too far into the technical jargon—and because Drupal has changed how it does site translations between its most recent versions—let's simply say that entity translation is a more automated translation process, whereas content translation provides more control by the site administrator. In line with their evaluation of Google Translate, Multnomah again chose the more focused approach of content translation.

In addition to guaranteeing that site visitors get correct information, page-specific translation means that no unintentional messages are sent. Jeremy explains this aspect: "A lot of content has no relevance in the translated language. We weren't going to lie to people: If a service, program, or item wasn't available in that language, we didn't translate it . . . We wanted to focus the user experience on critical items. One can realistically assume those using the site in these languages have a specific set of needs [that] probably didn't extend to reading old news releases, for example" (Graybill 2017). Jeremy admits that they didn't do any user testing with the specific language groups, but that would be another way to ensure that the content was providing the service you hope it will.

SUMMING UP

Once your library has publically stated its commitment to serving immigrants and new Americans through a statement or changes to your mission/vision, you can make your library more accessible to these populations by:

- Diversifying your staff, including for multilingualism
- Increasing staff empathy and cultural awareness
- Reducing language barriers in general
- Improving wayfinding through clear and/or translated signage
- Adding collections in relevant languages and with appropriate signage
- Providing relevant library and community information
- Increasing the overall usability of the library website
- Translating some or all of the website

The next five chapters examine how to develop programs and services for both newcomer and long-term residents that will help newcomers integrate and your community celebrate the diversity of cultures within its boundaries.

3

◇ ◇ ◇

LANGUAGE LITERACY
AND EDUCATION

One of the longest-running library services targeted at immigrants has been English language learning programs. From informal conversation groups to advanced English classes for the workplace, libraries have offered a neutral, free place for non-native speakers to practice hearing, speaking, and reading English.

Library English as a Second or Other Language (ESOL) programs are vital because they are free and, to some extent, easily expandable. Other low-cost programs quickly hit capacity and are often out of reach for those at the lowest economic levels. As Maddy Ildefonso of Los Angeles Public Library says, "ESL is something that we know that there's a need for; we are currently working on increasing our capacity. The adult schools are slammed. Community colleges are offering these classes, but not everybody can access them. We're trying to find a way to help those people who need further instruction and who can't access those traditional means" (Ildefonso 2017). Often, this means that even a very basic program at a library is better than nothing at all.

ENGLISH LANGUAGE LEARNING PROGRAMS

English language learning programs at the library can be as simple or as complex as the library's resources will support and as large and as diverse as the community needs. If your library isn't offering anything right now, starting with conversation groups and increasing complexity according to demand is probably the smartest choice. If you are offering something, consider expanding to augment what you're doing and meet unserved needs.

Over the past century, as libraries and educational providers formalized services to newcomers, several terms and acronyms were developed to describe both who's attending these programs and what their needs are, especially for language learning. There is an active conversation about the differences—both direct and implied—between the various names and acronyms for English learning environments. Without diving too deeply, here are the basics; ESOL will be used throughout this book, except when referring to an existing program. The following list of definitions is paraphrased from http://www.esltrail.com/2008/02/whats-difference-esl-efl-esol-ell-and.html (Hyte 2008):

- ESL = *English as a Second Language.* Used in English-speaking countries to describe programs in which non-English speakers can learn English.
- ESOL = *English as a Second or Other Language* or *English for Speakers of Other Languages.* Similar to ESL, but recognizes that many newcomers speak two or more languages fluently when they arrive.
- ESP = *English for Special Purposes.* Again, similar to ESL, but indicates that these programs are targeted at a specific field, usually for work or study purposes (e.g., English for medical professions).
- EFL = *English as a Foreign Language.* Used in non–English-speaking countries to describe places where native speakers can learn English.
- ELL = *English Language Learners.* Used in K–12 schools to describe non–English-fluent students.

Which should your library use? The best answer—and one repeated many times in this book—is to ask the people who know and care about these distinctions. If there are adult literacy organizations in your community, use the acronyms they use. If you know how many languages the "typical" newcomer speaks, choose between ESL and ESOL. If you want to be more inclusive, go with ESOL; if there are strong opinions in your area on why to use one or the other, find out what they are and whether they match the library's mission. Whatever term you choose, be consistent across all library programs, services, and signage so your users know that they're getting the same thing wherever they access your offerings.

Conversation Groups

Providing space and some structure is all that's really necessary to begin a conversation group. Like knitting groups, conversation groups can be entirely participant-run, but unlike those self-starting crafters, new English speakers often need support to participate fully. In most libraries, a staff member or a trained volunteer acts as facilitator and mentor during the conversation group, keeping tabs on the content of the discussion and making sure that no one dominates the conversation or acts in problematic ways.

The Boston Public Library has hosted English conversation groups for decades, always at the Central Library and as-needed at branch libraries. The format is the same: a volunteer prepares conversation topics and reference materials to have on hand, welcomes everyone as they arrive, and gets that day's conversation started. As participants talk together, the volunteer will answer questions, gently correct vocabulary and grammar, and keep the discussion flowing if it stalls. The group might talk about the same topic the entire time or allow tangents to lead them in fascinating new directions, according to the group's interests. Many participants come with questions about life in the United States, especially as they become regular attendees and understand what the conversation group has to offer them. At the end of the session, the volunteer answers final questions, might give some "homework" to encourage return visits, and points participants at community and library resources to meet needs that come up during the conversation.

Conversation group volunteers come from all parts of the community and are often, but not always, native English speakers. They receive basic training from library staff or other literacy workers in leading discussions, managing group dynamics and problematic behavior, and the library's resources for language learning and new community members. Later in the chapter, we'll look at possible sources for volunteers; if your library doesn't already have a formal volunteer program, ESOL programs can be a good pilot for one: they're targeted, with clearly bounded duties and responsibilities, and tend to run themselves once they've gotten going.

At the Boise Public Library, their groups are called Conversation Hours and began at the Hillcrest location, which has a high number of immigrants and refugees in the area. Sarah Kelley-Chase, formerly of the Hillcrest branch, explains: "We were looking for a way for people to get to know each other, have a relaxed space, and have an easy place to come chat about whatever they wanted to chat about while practicing English. There are some ground rules to it so that no one comes in and monopolizes the conversations, or comes in with a particular agenda because the idea is for it to be free conversation and practice. We have to vet volunteers to help facilitate it really well, with a sharp eye to make sure it's someone who'll come in and *just* be a facilitator. Because of paying close attention to who's in there, there's a fantastic core group of people over at Hillcrest who do a really great job facilitating and helping to recruit other volunteer facilitators. It's not uncommon to hear 5 or 6 different languages. Conversations run from a trip to the grocery store to something that happened on the news or the radio, something they overheard and are trying to make sense of it. And, of course, things like slang and vernacular and getting around town" (Kelley-Chase 2017).

Teaching What *Not* to Say

If you have a particularly good teacher, consider offering a class on English slang, swears, and offensive language and which contexts aren't appropriate for them, such as school or some workplaces. American English slang and swears can be very different than slang in other English variants and can benefit—and possibly amuse—even native speakers.

A variation on the standard conversation group is one focused on something particularly library relevant: books! The Rochester Hills (MI) Public Library has a four-session weekly ELL Book Discussion Group that combines practicing reading and conversation skills in the same program. The program description is upbeat and inviting: "Are you new to this country? Do you want to improve your English conversation skills? . . . At each session, the participants will read and discuss poems and short stories written in English. Together they will improve their English literacy skills while sharing traditions and cultures that celebrate our diversity" (Rochester Hills Public Library 2017).

Michelle Wisniewski, Oakland Talking Book Service Librarian, describes the beginning of the club: "Our original conversation group was modeled after a similar program at the Seattle Public Library called Talk Time. On one of the earliest handouts, we specified our goals:

- Improve and enhance the English literacy skills of participants
- Expose participants to various types of literature
- Enrich and expand friendships
- Share traditions and cultures and celebrate diversity

All of our conversation groups focus on the last two bullets and are primarily facilitated by staff persons who are multilingual and have personal immigrant life experience" (Wisniewski 2017).

When staff at Rochester Hills came up with the idea of an immigrant-focused book discussion group, they asked local educator Elana Izraeli, PhD, to facilitate. Her background as a reading specialist made her a perfect fit. Says Michelle, "Dr. Izraeli incorporates the four elements of reading strategies into the Newcomers group: speech, reading, writing and listening. At the beginning of each session, she distributes a questionnaire that provides insight into the participant's goals and current English literacy. She selects poems, short stories and at times, brief novels that are appropriate for the group" (Wisniewski 2017). Correcting another person's pronunciation is discouraged; the focus is on being more comfortable reading aloud and speaking with ease.

The Newcomers' Book Club meets on Thursdays from 10 to 11:30 a.m. to discuss poetry, American short stories, and the news. Attendance ranges from 10 to 20 participants and tends to be highly educated women with strong English skills. Participants come from many countries, including France, Japan, Cuba, and China. Discussion centers around English language writers that many participants had never heard of—Frost, Angelou, Kipling, Dickens—and occasionally the group doesn't even get through a full paragraph because they "are deep into discussion, and everyone's bringing his or her background knowledge," Izraeli says (Izraeli 2017).

The club also explores skills beyond reading. For U.S. holidays, members bring in home-cooked dishes to discuss their cultural significance. Members also write poems that are bound into books that they can take home. "Every opportunity I have to make them express themselves and talk and present, I use it," says Izraeli (Izraeli 2017).

This broad-based approach extends the benefits well past reading and conversational skills. Says, Michelle, "[My library career] has included public programming as well as driving a 26-foot bookmobile through ice and snow. The ELL groups have been one of my most rewarding work experiences—I have traveled around the world without leaving the library" (Wisniewski 2017). Her sentiment is echoed by a participant, Lucia Pieri: "It's very easy to have friends because all of us are foreigners, and we need to know each other. There are people all over the world, and in other situations, you wouldn't have the opportunity to talk and learn" (Diaz 2016).

English Language Classes

Moving up a notch from conversation groups, formal classes in English provide structured environments for more consistent and deeper learning. English classes can range from "New Arrival Survival English" to advanced topics in specific fields and can be either drop-in or registration-based. Courses often run for a specific length of time on a monthly or quarterly basis, and participants are encouraged to attend all sessions.

Structurally, English classes follow the same guidelines as any other learning: the teacher uses a combination of lecture and practice to teach a set curriculum, with stated learning goals and markers of achievement for students. Lessons might be more or less participatory, depending on the teaching style, but as with most adult basic education (ABE), they always relate to something in the learners' daily lives. Even more than with children, adults learn best by linking their new skill to a practical need; teaching parts of speech and sentence structure without a purpose will not be useful to adult English language learners.

The San José Public Library works with the various resources of its branches and community needs to provide some form of ESOL instruction at most locations. At the Seventrees Branch Library's Family Learning Center classroom, Coordinator Cristina (Cris) Johnson (MA, TESL) has a structured series of classes ranging from absolute beginner to advanced. "I offer a variety of classes to suit various students' literacy levels," says Cris (Johnson 2017). Each class has an overall concept: listening/speaking, reading/writing, pronunciation, grammar, or vocabulary. Two different program descriptions give a better sense of the range of classes:

> "ESL Class Level 1 Beginning Clear Speech Red Book 1: In this class students will participate in activities to improve fluency and speaking skills" (San José Public Library n.d. B).
> "ESL Class Level 5 Advance Reading, Reading Concepts 4: Students will read special selection [sic] of classic American authors to identify topics, learn to read for comprehension and skim, and practice evaluating information" (San José Public Library n.d. C).

In contrast, the Dr. Roberto Cruz Alum Rock Branch Library (usually called the Alum Rock Branch) in San José partners with a local adult education program to "provide English language learner practice with reading, writing, and speaking skills to prepare for work or citizenship" (San José Public Library n.d. A). Beyond the beginners class, the Alum Rock Branch gears its English learning primarily towards citizenship preparation through practice classes. We'll look more closely at citizenship and work-place language skills in later chapters.

In addition to the library examples, seek out local adult education providers and see how they do it. For example, the Cambridge (MA) Center for Adult Education includes English language skills classes at multiple levels and with different goals, which all proceed along a path (see Table 3.1).

Although your library's ESOL classes don't need to be as comprehensive or varied as this—the Alum Rock Branch does well with just a couple of offerings—if you're offering a large number of classes, it can be helpful to organize them by level. You can let students self-select their level, or you can include an assessment as part of a registration process, if you have enough students to need one. Remember, once a student is in a class, the instructor should be evaluating them and can recommend they move up or down a level if needed.

Table 3.1: ESOL Class Titles from the Cambridge (MA) Center for Adult Education

Beginner	Intermediate	Advanced
Integrated Skills: Beginners 1–4	Integrated Skills: Intermediate	Comparative Literature
Basic English for Everyday Life (greetings, identifying the things and people of daily life)	English for Everyday Life: Intermediate	Advanced Pronunciation
Conversation for Beginners	Intermediate Speech and Discussion Workshop	Preparation for the TOEFL
	Intermediate Conversation	Intensive Preparation for the TOEFL
	Intermediate Writing	Read, Discuss, Debate!
	Pronunciation Practice	Advanced Speech and Presentation Workshop
	Public Speaking and Presentation	Advanced Writing and Grammar
	Reading and Understanding Humor in American Culture	

Note: For more information, visit http://www.ccae.org.

Table 3.2: Digest of Rubric from User Dluisa at Rcampus, Powered by iRubric

	Beginner	Low Intermediate	High Intermediate	Advanced
Speaking	Low-level words and erratic sentence structure and grammar	Phrases, sometimes forgets subjects/ pronouns, wrong verb tenses	Good fluency, good sentence structure with pauses, easy to understand	Fluently with good grammar and sentence structure, self-correcting and clear
Listening	Understands 15% of content	30%	45%	90%
Reading	Understands 15% of content	30%	45%	90%
Writing	Many errors, no organized or coherent writing	Fair grammar with quite a few errors, poorly organized content	Good grammar with few errors, reasonably well-organized content	Excellent grammar with minimal errors and very organized content
Comprehension	Can't explain what they've read or show understanding	Can explain the general idea in a clear way	Can explain a summary of what's been read or seen with good organization	Can explain a summary with excellent detail and organization
Grammar	Uses correct verb tense 15% of the time	30%	45%	90%

Note: See the full version at http://www.rcampus.com/rubricshowc.cfm?code=Q522CA&sp=yes.

Many ESOL assessment rubrics are available online or in existing ESOL instructor materials, but the clearest example I found comes from Rcampus' iRubric platform (see Table 3.2).

Tutors and Other 1:1 Learning Programs

If your library doesn't have the demand to justify full classes, if you want to offer more individual support, or if your intended audience can't make scheduled classes, tutor programs, using either professional tutors or volunteers, are an excellent option. Individual tutoring can be both an easier and harder program to maintain: there are more people to manage in terms of both tutors and students, but it can make it easier to guarantee that the timing will be perfect for each individual student and improve success rates and overall attendance.

Like any volunteer program, more oversight is required for a tutoring program than for classes. Library staff need to recruit volunteers, recruit students, come up with some kind of matching system to put them together, and help the pairs keep track of their schedules, especially if they need to reserve library space for each session. Each library should determine its own needs in terms of the level of pedagogy involved; for example, should the tutoring sessions be more like a conversation group or more like a formal class?

Informal Individual Learning

At the Louisville Free Public Library's Iroquois branch, they've opted for a conversational approach. Developed by Sophie Maier, the English Conversation Club (ECC) brings together "helpers" (more on this later in the chapter) and learners in 1:1 sessions, filling up a program room and occasionally spilling out into the hallway. Participants can be new arrivals or longer-term residents who are at a point where they can concentrate on learning English. The local community college has many refugee and immigrant students who have finished an English learning program but sometimes need additional support with research or editing papers. Other participants include children and young adults who need homework help or those studying for certification exams.

One of the ECC's longtime helpers is Kate Cunningham, a friend of Sophie's mother Donna. She got involved because "Donna said, Sophie's put together this English Conversation Club on Saturdays at the library. Would you be interested? Because she knew that I had done ESL as a volunteer in previous years." Ten years later, Kate is still volunteering, as is Donna.

Kate describes how the ECC program works: "It's just a pick-up team of volunteers, different people every week. It [can be] a little funny, because you talk to somebody who wants information about the riverfront park and you bring that the next week and you never see that person again! But at least you have the information there in case anyone else asks about the park." Carts of library materials, flash cards, sign-in materials, and general homework and tutor supplies (pens, paper, etc.) are stationed at the sign-in desk and inside the program room. Maps of Louisville and the world help orient helpers and learners on where they come from and where they are. Adds Kate, "Quite often, it's the community volunteers who'll say, Oh, she's from Belarus . . . where's Belarus? And then we pull out the map."

Kate has dozens of stories from her decade with ECC: "One time I was talking to a young man—I wish I could remember his name, it was such an unusual name—and he was from Micronesia. It turns out his brother-in-law was also in the room [and later, he introduced us]. I said 'Hello, how are you?' And the brother-in-law said he was from Guam! I asked how it was possible that he could be from Micronesia and the brother-in-law was from Guam. And the brother-in-law said, 'Well, I'm from Micronesia too but nobody knows where that is, they're more likely to know where Guam is, so I just say I'm from Guam!' They're both in the middle of the Pacific somewhere, but at least we've heard of Guam and it's easier to spell" (Cunningham 2017).

Saturday morning at the ECC follows a standard schedule: people sign in on a list for learners or for helpers, and both receive a name badge with their first name, printed clearly by the sign-in team. (They tried having participants write their names, but decided it was more effective for the helpers to do it.) The badges are collected as a rudimentary "inventory" and deter the kids from the library who try to run in and grab refreshments.

As people arrive, learners and helpers are matched, usually by Sophie, who seems to know everyone. Helpers rarely work with the same person two weeks in a row unless they're working on a special project; one volunteer, Bill, worked for several Saturdays with a young physician to prepare for the United States Medical Licensing Exam in Chicago. (We'll tell this story in our chapter on workforce development.) Conversational prompts and starter questions ranging from basic to advanced are at another table and include seasonal or local topics of interest like horse racing and the Kentucky Derby. By asking basic questions—"How long have you been in Louisville?" "Where do you live?"—helpers determine what level the learner is at and can then start asking more specific questions about what the learner is interested in or needs to do for the rest of the session.

Although it can seem disjointed to have random helpers and learners each week, it's also a benefit, Kate stresses. "Part of it is getting people to converse with people who have various ways of speaking. [In the late 1990s, I was working with a group of Cubans who had just arrived.] Their English was good, but they had learned very formally and they would ask me, 'Is that a present participle? Would you use the present participle there?' Well, yes, you would, but I'm going to be one of the only people you'll ever meet who knows what a participle is. Also, they had come by way of the airport in Cincinnati, and whoever was speaking on the various PA system . . . they couldn't understand [the voices]. So they were so afraid that after all of their studying, they wouldn't be able to understand anybody [in the United States]. When they came to the classroom and they could understand me, they were greatly relieved" (Cunningham 2017).

A Highly Structured Approach

In contrast, the San José Public Library's (SJPL) Partners in Reading (PAR) adult and family literacy program, established in 1989, includes a very formal tutoring program for both native-born and newcomer residents. The PAR program also includes the ESL classes we've already looked at, and the tutoring program is available as a next step. Volunteer PAR tutors, trained by staff, instruct adult learners in reading, writing, and computer skills based on the learner's self-established goals. When a new learner signs up for the program, a Literacy Program Specialist assesses them and matches them with a tutor.

PAR tutors go through an extensive training program, beginning with a 90-minute orientation and continuing in two 6-hour training sessions, before being placed with a learner. Requirements to be a PAR tutor include being 18 years or older, fluency in English with a high school diploma or GED, acquiring "fingerprint clearance" (in other states, this might include a criminal background check or CORI [Criminal Offender Record Information]), and being of a certain temperament: "have patience, flexibility, cultural sensitivity, enthusiasm and a sense of humor" (San José Public Library n.d. E). Tutors agree to a minimum commitment of three hours per week for at least six months and to meet in the library or another public place. In return, the library provides extensive instructional materials and support through tutor meetings, workshops, and individual work with the literacy program specialists. An example of what a mature, robust tutoring program could look like, SJPL's PAR program seeks to fulfill its promise that tutors will feel "the satisfaction of helping your community grow stronger by helping adults build their literacy skills," making personal connections and knowing they've made a difference in an adult's life (San José Public Library n.d. E).

Part of the support PAR tutors receive is via the library's website. On the PAR Tutor Resources page (http://www.sjpl.org/partutorresources), tutors have access to suggested lesson plans, reporting documents, tips and suggestions, a link to the PAR Learner Resource page, an extensive list of links to other tutor support websites, and tips from previous PAR tutors. Even after the official training, PAR tutors are given plenty of resources to help themselves and their tutees succeed.

Scheduling

There are many tools you can use to coordinate tutoring pairs. A simple Google or Microsoft calendar may be all you need, as long as whoever does the schedule can make changes to the calendar, and it can be publicly available so the tutor pairs can see it on their own. If your library has event scheduling software that includes a registration field, you can use it for tutoring; in the LibGuides suite of apps from Springshare, you can use LibCal to schedule individual tutoring sessions in the same way as appointments with staff. There are dozens of online and software-based tutor scheduling programs, with price dictating the number of features you get. It's a good idea to get recommendations from educational organizations or existing tutors you trust, but take a look at these for a general sense of features and pricing:

- Oases, http://www.oasesonline.com
- TeachWorks, http://teachworks.com
- TutorCruncher, http://tutorcruncher.com
- TutorPanel, http://www.tutorpanel.com
- Also look at business-focused programs like SetATime (http://setatime.co)

Tech Tools

As a supplement to in-person classes or to provide a service that goes beyond the library building, libraries can provide or recommend technology tools to help ESOL learners.

Most library-subscription language learning programs include ESOL modules, as do popular online or app-based programs like Duolingo (http://www.duolingo.com). Use your library website to collect and promote these tools, either on pages for ESOL learners themselves or on support pages for instructors, facilitators, and tutors. The following list is just a starting point and includes general learning resources that have modules specifically useful for ESOL learners.

- **Language Learning:**
  - Brainfuse
  - Mango Languages

- ○ Muzzy, which is explicitly for children
- ○ Pimsleur, including a version for children called Little Pim
- ○ PowerSpeak
- ○ Pronunciator
- ○ Transparent Language Online
- **General Learning Platforms:**
  - ○ LearningExpress Library includes English instruction for native speakers and citizenship test preparation/green card instructions in English and Spanish
  - ○ Gale Courses and Career Online High School
  - ○ GCFLearnFree.org: well known for its basic computer skills training, it also has ESOL reading instruction

Cell phones and other mobile devices can extend learning even further. The Los Angeles Public Library uses a program called Cell-Ed to provide text message–based ESOL instruction to anyone with a library card. Alicia Moguel, Associate Director of Lifelong Learning, explains, "Basically, people who have jobs at various hours or multiple jobs, they don't have time to come in to a conventional conversation circle [or other library-based program]. We encourage anyone who wants to begin ESL instruction but can't find the time to attend an adult school or come in to a literacy center to start there" (Moguel 2017). Using a combination of text messages, pre-recorded lessons, and live coaches, Cell-Ed provides instruction in English language literacy, Spanish reading literacy, job and life skills, and pre–high school and college preparation. The company uses national education standards to guide their instruction goals and includes assessments and surveys to measure effectiveness. Partner organizations who work with Cell-Ed can receive reports on the progress their users make, which helps with making the case for additional funding (see "Making the Case" in Chapter 8). Visit http://www.cell-ed.com for more information.

Family Literacy

Many immigrants and refugees, especially women, come to the library with children and elders. These multigenerational families are well served by Family Learning Centers and programs that offer materials and activities for all ages, sometimes in simultaneous separate programs for children and adults/caregivers. San José Public Library established Family Learning Centers in seven branch libraries approximately 12 years ago to address the needs of neighborhoods with combinations of low income, low literacy, and immigration among residents.

Each Family Learning Center (FLC) has dedicated staff, facilities, special collections, and technology and offers free programs and services to families and individuals ranging from life skills to literacy. Currently, the program focuses on citizenship preparation, English language, literacy, parenting, and basic life skills.

"Each FLC has a Literacy Program Specialist who strives to make branches less intimidating and more welcoming to the immigrant community," says San José Public Library Director Jill Bourne. "These FLC Coordinators take on the responsibility of understanding the needs of their surrounding communities through both formal and informal mechanisms, such as community conversations, surveys, getting to know customers locally, partnering with community-based organizations. This allows the coordinator to have a deep understanding of community rhythms and build a solid rapport/trust with other stakeholders within the community" (Bourne 2017). Through partnerships, volunteers, or designing/leading themselves, coordinators develop programs, events, and information tables to meet those specific needs.

Events and highlights of the Family Learning Centers include:

- Parenting classes and workshops
- ESL and citizenship classes
- Bilingual story times
- ESL conversation clubs
- Computer instruction in multiple languages
- Informational programs in diverse languages
- Cultural programs in representative languages
- Computers with software for ESL, typing, and language acquisition
- Collections of books, videos, DVDs, and multimedia kits on ESL, citizenship, basic life skills, literacy, and GED and other test preparation

The Boise Public Library partners with a local family literacy program called Learning Lab to offer services at all locations; Learning Lab has a dedicated space at the Central Library and conductions additional programs at the branches. Sarah Kelley-Chase of the Bown Crossing location describes an event she was planning with support from Learning Lab: "We're working with a local housing complex building manager to host a

BBQ at the complex, and have members of the Learning Lab there" along with representatives from the library.

In a more typical scenario, Learning Lab conducts literacy classes for adults, incorporating the children, immediately preceding the library's usual Tiny Explorers story time. This allows time for kids and adults to interact and still get some literacy skills through storytelling as well as individual play.

The Library! at Bown Crossing (the branch's official title) was only open for a few months when "requests began to roll in for a program similar to the English Corner conversation groups," adds Sarah. "We're not too far away from Micron, which is a large company with a number of employees from overseas, especially different places in Asia. Those aren't refugees, but not really immigrants either. The families don't stay all that long—they might stay a few years and then go back—but they have a lot of requests for English proficiency, which will make for an interesting mix when we're able to get something up and going" (Kelley-Chase 2017).

Language Sharing

Language sharing workshops are different from any of the programs mentioned earlier because the exchange is frequently two-way: native English speakers help nonspeakers with their English while also learning or improving their understanding of the other's language. Frequently done in 1:1 sessions, language sharing opportunities can be brokered by the library and then left to run themselves, or they can be overseen more directly by library staff. Because the English speaker usually has some understanding of the other language, it's easier for them to be self-sustaining in terms of schedule and resources.

Group language sharing opportunities can resemble conversation groups, but where the point of an English conversation group is to practice English, conversations in multiple languages are the goal of a language sharing conversation program. The same participant might move from a cluster of people having an English discussion about local resources, to a group talking about soccer/fútbol in Spanish, to simply listening to an Arabic conversation to hear how the language sounds.

Language sharing opportunities are often volunteer programs, with matchmaking overseen by the library. After that, the pairs or groups can set their own schedule and meet inside or outside the library as desired; coffee shops are frequent destinations for language sharing pairs. The library continues to support the learners with resources, but the work happens entirely between the participants.

At the Multnomah County Library, however, the library has an official language exchange program for English and Spanish speakers. Intercambio meetings are typically on weekend days at a few branches and provide a space for learners at all levels to practice both languages in a casual atmosphere. Participants interact as a large group, speaking half the time in English and the other half in Spanish, and the calendar event for the program includes the description in both languages (Multnomah n.d.).

Whether you want to try a 1:1 or group program, language sharing programs benefit from outreach to local high schools or colleges, encouraging students to come to the library and connect with other students or adults who speak the language they're studying through conversation practice/immersion. Your ESOL learners benefit from the English practice, and language students benefit from out-of-classroom conversational experience.

Accent and Idiom Work

Once learners have mastered the basics, they often seek out programs on accent reduction and pronunciation to improve the clarity of their speech. General accent reduction practice can come through a conversation group where participants get feedback on how they pronounce words in context, giving participants the option to drift into side discussions and explore ideas more thoroughly. Alternatively, classes can focus on any of the subject areas mentioned in the "English for Specific Purposes" section later. For example, a class on the pronunciation of school-related terms could help parents interact more effectively with teachers and administrators. (We'll look more closely at workplace-related needs in Chapter 5.)

Another possibility is to zoom in on American idioms. As mentioned previously, we use many colloquialisms in the United States, and they vary wildly from one part of the country to another. Immigrants who learned basic English in the Northeast states might be struggling to understand Midwestern slang. A class on regional idioms and colloquialisms can improve the daily life of many newcomers, and participants can discuss how language differs within the United States to help them if they need to move to another part of the country. These classes might be best taught by trained volunteers, professional instructors, or library staff, due to the comparative research required to correctly identify regional differences of American English. However, if you wanted to spotlight local slang and phrases, a long-term resident volunteer—given some parameters—would be an excellent choice. See also the Brainstorm Box on swears and possibly offensive language earlier in this chapter.

Although local community members might be the best source for local colloquialisms, there are some resources that can help you put together idiom-focused programs:

- *Speaking American*, Josh Katz, Houghton Mifflin Harcourt, 2016
- Dictionary of American Regional English (DARE), www.daredictionary.com
- Dictionaries of idiom and slang from Oxford, Farlex, NTC, and McGraw-Hill

English for Specific Purposes

You can insert English for Specific Purposes (ESP) sessions into any level or type of English language learning your library offers. From "Survival English" to "Advanced Daily Life," classes on everyday words are immediately useful to all participants. A focused class or specific tutors that specialize in everyday English can bring newcomers up to speed quickly, more than the general topics of bigger classes.

Topic-specific classes, conversation groups, or tutoring sessions can also fill identified needs. Food and dining, shopping, education, Internet/computer terms, and health/medical terms would all be excellent focal points of a class. Depending on who your participants are, more awkward topics like sex, religion, and politics might be useful discussion topics, but be very aware of highly different societal norms among countries of origin, especially regarding human body functions and sexual mores. See the resources in the section on cultural awareness in Chapter 2 for more on these differences.

(In Chapter 4, we'll look at citizenship interview practice programs, and in Chapter 5, we'll look more closely at English learning for workplace-related needs.)

NATIVE LANGUAGE LITERACY

One last area to explore is offering literacy programs in whatever the most common languages are among newcomers in your area other than English. This isn't something many libraries are doing at this time, either due to the diversity of language needs or the lack of interest on the part of their communities, so it's worth exploring whether these programs are needed by your residents before starting to develop them.

That said, a group often overlooked in language services to newcomers is new arrivals from English-speaking countries with limited literacy in written English. In addition to the West Indies/Caribbean, arrivals from countries in Europe and Africa, India, and Australia where English is an official language may need the same kind of adult basic education programs as U.S.-born residents with low literacy—they can speak well, but read below an "average" adult level. Homa Naficy of Hartford Public Library says, "When we were building our citizenship program, we have, over the past few years, encountered many folks from the West Indies who are fluent in spoken English, but have no/low reading/writing skills. We've made an extra effort to focus in that area," she adds, but it can be a challenge to attract funders to these programs because the need isn't as immediately obvious. Homa continues, "People often think of immigrants and ESL, but then you have folks like the West Indian community and staff are never sure [of their needs]. They speak fluent English but they can't read and write; it's never portrayed that way" in accounts of what newcomers require for integration (Naficy 2017).

Another tension can be an unanticipated outcome of increasing accommodations to reach people in their native language: removing the pressure to learn English. Homa has experienced this firsthand in Hartford: "One of the challenges I see with the Spanish language, it's hard to learn English because everything is in Spanish. We have a large Spanish-speaking community . . . and everything is in Spanish. Your credit card form is in Spanish, your doctor is in Spanish, your banker is in Spanish. The two hours or six hours that you're coming to learn English, if that's the only exposure you get, then it's virtually impossible for an older Spanish-speaking person living in a city or town that is highly Spanish-speaking to learn English. We tell students, 'Watch or listen to an English channel. How can you learn if you go back and watch Telemundo all day?'" Homa also encourages multilingual library staff to speak English to people they know are lawful permanent residents working towards citizenship, including through the library's own programs. "They have to have that English to pass. They're not going to pass if you keep speaking Spanish to them. After they have their citizenship, then that's fine" (Naficy 2017).

One exception to this need to speak English for the citizenship test has arisen due to the extremely high number of native Spanish speakers living in the United States, many for decades as lawful permanent residents, who are only now taking their citizenship exams. People who have lived in the United States with a green card for 20 years who are ages 50 and older, and for 15 years who are ages 55 and older, can sit for the citizenship exam in their own language because it's harder to learn English at this point. Hartford offers a citizenship class in Spanish to serve these not-as-new Americans, often with more than 30 participants in each session.

If you decide to create literacy or citizenship programs in languages other than English at your library, the challenge becomes the diversity of regional dialects in those languages and, potentially, the lack of a written form of the language. In some countries, written language is a product of the late 20th century and both globalization and colonialism, such as the Bantu languages of Africa mentioned in Chapter 2. Older non-English speakers may feel no need to be fluent in a written form that didn't exist when they were younger, and younger newcomers may strongly prefer to focus on their English literacy to integrate quickly into their new country. Again, this is an opportunity to reach out to the community and relevant organizations to find out what the needs of your local residents are.

WHO'S IN CHARGE?

For any of these programs, the oversight and provision requirements should be different from library to library, because the needs of the community and staff abilities and resources vary tremendously from place to place. In the earlier sections, we touch on what kinds of structure might work for different types of programs, but let's take a more general look at the pluses and minuses of each type of leader/tutor/teacher.

Staff

Depending on your library's resources, it might be both possible and preferable for library staff to lead whatever English language learning programs you offer. It's easier to keep a higher standard and consistency of the teaching if the same people are providing it, and it's easier to monitor that quality if library staff are the ones doing the teaching. Coordinating staff removes the occasional unpredictability of working with volunteers, even the most dedicated folks, and can create an instant pool of substitutes if a staff member has a last-minute emergency. If you have staff members eager to lead these programs, that's certainly a reason to let them run with it; in contrast, a lack of staff interest would be a reason to use volunteers or paid instructors.

The obvious downside of this approach is the potential for "yet another thing" to ask overloaded staff to do. Unless there is a high-level reassessment that changes library priorities to this kind of service—replacing outdated programs with English language learning sessions—staff won't be able to give these programs the attention they deserve and need for success. Current staff may also not be comfortable working with non–English-speaking patrons in situations that require more depth than basic library interactions; unless they're given extensive training and support, they may not be the most effective facilitators for these programs.

Volunteers

Volunteer programs continue to be a struggle in libraries because of the oversight and training needed to establish volunteers in the library, increased security vetting requirements (background checks, etc.) for anyone interacting with the public, or disagreements over limits on job responsibilities between different kinds of library staff. Although a deep discussion of these topics is outside the scope of this book, a few points are closely related to the kinds of programs and services needed by newcomers.

If your library already has a volunteer program, adding services that utilize volunteers can be straightforward. If your library doesn't, then an English language learning program can be a good pilot for one: they're targeted, with clearly bounded duties and responsibilities, and tend to run themselves once they've gotten going. Also, the duties don't typically overlap with existing staff duties at any level, so it might be easier for more traditional libraries to introduce the idea. Creative labeling can also help reduce tensions and indicate the restrictions around a volunteer's role. For the Louisville Public Library's English Conversation Club sessions, they use the term "helper" rather than "volunteer" to show the limited scope of what ECC helpers do: they help English language learners practice, and that's it.

The time and effort of training and managing volunteers present another challenge for libraries, but as seen in several of our examples, once a training program is set up, it becomes a routine part of the library's work. As new volunteers come on board, they receive a standard level of training offered for that program, depending on their existing skills. For very informal programs like the English Conversation Club at the Iroquois branch in Louisville, they don't provide any training but offer support to new helpers; the high variability of who volunteers to help each Saturday precludes any more intensive training. For other conversation groups, this training might be in basic group management, the library's resources, and conversation prompts to keep things moving. More formal classes and tutoring, such as at San José's Partners in Reading program, offer additional adult literacy training through workshops and online support.

In the previous section on ESOL tutoring, different approaches to scheduling and managing tutors were discussed; these same tools can be used to register new volunteers for training purposes, or trainings can be drop-in to reduce the oversight needed.

Professionals

If your library is rich in resources, either through partnership opportunities or funding, you have the option of using ESOL instructors with advanced training for learning programs. Both San José and Boise public libraries work with adult education providers and exchange space for services. Another possibility is tapping into local colleges with education majors who are looking for student intern or practicum placement, who might work with you to give their students real-world teaching experience.

Hiring professional outside instructors using program budgets or grant funding has the primary advantage of being entirely self-run English learning programs that just need scheduling and promotion to put the word out. These instructors may have accreditation as teachers of English as a second or other language, and often come with their own curriculum and teaching process. It's possible that some may offer pro bono services to a library, but equally possible that they will require a reasonable fee for the programs; search for local providers for a better sense of costs in your area.

Community or Participant Led

For conversation groups and any 1:1 situation, it's possible for participants to directly structure their own experience. In groups, long-time participants occasionally come to take on a facilitator role, encouraging newcomers and directing the conversation if the native English-speaking volunteer is helping an individual. They may, over time, become the volunteer leading the group; many do once their fluency is sufficient to give back to the program that helped them get there.

In 1:1 learning such as tutoring and language sharing, after they are matched by the library, the two participants can set their own meeting schedule and topics of interest so as to better serve their individual needs. Tutor pairs might work from a library-provided program curriculum, but they have much more flexibility in terms of tangents and focus.

Finding Instructors and Volunteers

This topic is examined more closely in Chapters 6 and 7, but with ESOL programs there seem to be two primary sources for facilitators: individual volunteers and partnerships with adult literacy organizations.

As previously mentioned, Louisville works exclusively under the volunteer model, most directly brought in by Sophie Maier's efforts. Helper Kate Cunningham says the most common question at the sign-in desk is, "Do you know Sophie?" Her Conversation Club helpers are community residents, older volunteers who know either Sophie or her mother Donna, and college professors and students whose classes Sophie visits as a guest lecturer. "I go and give a spiel about who are the immigrants and refugees of Louisville," Sophie says, "then tweak it to fit whatever discipline [the class is in]. I do this in exchange for the professor to make it mandatory [for their students] to come help, if we want them to, preferably multiple times. Those have brought in a large crowd, both of community folk and also educators who are constantly striving to be more culturally competent in the classroom. That's been nifty."

Sophie's relationship with the universities is, therefore, mutually beneficial. The library gets interns and helpers, and students may practice a language they're learning and are exposed to diverse cultures . . . and the library. Says Sophie, "In our private, affluent university, folks have often had very little contact with the public library since they were children, so they get a message about the relevance of the public library. At our community college, we have a lot of low-income U.S.-born folks, veterans, with kids or who are working full time, who might otherwise not engage with the foreign-born community. It usually produces a pretty lovely outcome, if I do say so myself" (Maier 2017).

SUMMING UP

From a weekly conversation circle to an assessment-based system of formal English classes, English language learning at the library can truly come in all types and sizes. When you determine what level of effort your library can sustain and what the needs of your immigrant communities are, you can find a way to balance these in whatever program you have or create.

Whether it's staff led or volunteer facilitated, English learning at the library tends to take one of the following forms:

- Conversation groups
- English classes
- 1:1 instruction
- Language sharing

These programs might focus on basic English, advanced topics in reading and writing, accent and idiom practice, family literacy, or special topics related to life or work. A wide variety of tech tools—including app-based or subscription learning platforms—can augment in-person programs and services to make English language learning available to all who need it, regardless of schedule and financial ability.

The next chapter will address the second-most important need of many newcomers: information on and preparation for the U.S. citizenship process.

4

◇ ◇ ◇

CITIZENSHIP

For many newcomers, after accessibility to basic services and English language learning, a path to citizenship is the next priority. Not all people from other countries are immigrating, but for those who are choosing to relocate to the United States permanently, the library can be a primary source of information and support for the process of becoming a U.S. citizen. In this chapter, you'll learn how libraries are providing that support, from providing information to staff- and resource-intensive legal aid assistance programs.

CITIZENSHIP MATERIALS

From a single shelf to a dedicated display area, libraries can usually find some space to make citizenship materials available. Basic citizenship information includes:

- "Know Your Rights": a list of the three most important personal rights for citizens (more on this in the next section)
- Information and forms on how to apply for a green card or citizenship
- A list of local resources for applicants, including ESOL classes

If you have additional space, continue to add to your citizenship materials from the list in the "Citizenship Corners" section later.

Know Your Rights

In 2016, Los Angeles Public Library immediately responded to the changing political climate around the presidential election by prominently displaying links to "Know Your Rights" information on their website home page. The need for this information continues to be vitally important, and providing information online and in physical form can be a lifesaver for someone approached by federal or local agents.

In partnership with the Immigrant Legal Resource Center (ILRC), the Fresno County Public Library is providing "Red Cards:" a wallet-sized red plastic card in English and Spanish that lists the three most important personal rights to remember if someone is detained by any type of officer:

- Remain silent
- Don't sign anything
- Don't open the door without a warrant signed by a judge

Making these cards available helps increase their knowledge of their rights as residents in the United States and helps them keep themselves and their families safe during interactions with officials. Learn more about the "Know Your Rights" campaign at:

- National Immigration Law Center: http://www.nilc.org/issues /immigration-enforcement
- American Civil Liberties Union (ACLU): http://www.aclu.org /know-your-rights
- The National Lawyers Guild (NLG): http://nlg.org/know-your -rights
- Los Angeles Public Library: http://www.lapl.org/citizenship/know -your-rights

Citizenship Corners

Since 2013, the Institute of Museum and Library Services (IMLS) has worked with the United States Citizenship and Immigration Services (USCIS) to help libraries provide accurate and useful information about citizenship to potential applicants through staff training and materials provided for free or low cost. In this section, we'll look at the essentials of a Citizenship Corner; for more information on the history of the project and detailed resources, visit the USCIS page on Citizenship Corners at http://uscis.gov/citizenship/organizations/libraries.

Recognizing that libraries vary wildly, USCIS provides a set of guidelines designed to fit Citizenship Corners into whatever space a library has available, from a single shelf or display to an entire room. Citizenship Corner materials might include (USCIS n.d. A):

- Materials available from USCIS:
  - *Learn About the United States: Quick Civics Lessons for the Naturalization Test*
  - Vocabulary flash cards for the naturalization test
  - Civics Flash Cards for the Naturalization Test (English and Spanish)
  - Copies of Form N-400, Application for Naturalization
  - Citizenship awareness posters in English, Chinese, Spanish, and Vietnamese
  - Informational flyers in English, Chinese, Spanish, and Vietnamese highlighting naturalization eligibility requirements and resources available on the USCIS website
- The brochure *10 Steps to Naturalization: Understanding the Process of Becoming a U.S. Citizen*
- Books and magazines from your collections that "address questions on the naturalization test, such as famous Americans, historical events, and important founding documents" (USCIS n.d. A)
- Information about ESOL and citizenship classes at the library
- Lists of local resources helpful to newcomers, including legal aid for citizenship and other organizations that offer language and citizenship classes (USCIS n.d. A)

The USCIS stresses that Citizenship Corners should remain focused on the citizenship process; if your Corner is small or you have extensive existing ESOL or test preparation sections, display signage pointing users to related materials elsewhere in the library.

To help libraries start their Citizenship Corners, they can register to receive one free *Civics and Citizenship Toolkit* through the USCIS website; the Toolkit is composed of immigration and civics publications, handbooks, multimedia tools, and a quick-start guide. It was designed to "make it easier for organizations to provide basic information to immigrant communities, develop content for classes, and train staff and volunteers" (USCIS n.d. B).

When possible, libraries have added dedicated monitor displays or computers to their Citizenship Corners, and others staff their Corners with trained volunteers. If your small screen is attached to a simple computer, it can repeatedly show a short informational video about the naturalization process; touchscreen monitors or tablets on stands can be set to display the USCIS Citizen Resource Center website, including online videos describing the process and reviewing for the test. Volunteers who are available in the Corners can answer basic questions, point people to specific resources, and help applicants navigate the Citizenshipworks website (see next section). Uncertified volunteers may not offer any advanced citizenship help, including answering detailed questions about the application process, but representatives from recognized and accredited organizations may. The particulars of what constitutes legal aid and the Department of Justice recognition and accreditation process are discussed at the end of this chapter.

In December 2015, the Fresno County Public Library installed six Citizenship Corners; there are currently Corners in 18 branches, plus the Bookmobile; the ultimate goal is to have a Corner in every location. Each Citizenship Corner contains study materials in multiple languages, circulating flashcards and DVDs, and a set of reference books in several languages on aspects of immigration and naturalization. Community Librarian Michelle Gordon adds, "In addition to the physical spaces, we overhauled our online presence on the subject. There is a great pathfinder with local resources and links to more study materials" (Gordon 2017).

The USCIS Citizenship Corner page offers additional resources for libraries, including suggestions on what materials to put out and how to display them. For more information, visit http://www.uscis.gov/citizenship/organi zations/libraries/citizenship-corners.

CITIZENSHIP EVENTS

Hosting a citizenship event can be a way to introduce the library to new Americans and is often less staff intensive than any other event. Working with a local USCIS office, libraries can use their meeting rooms or auditoriums as a location for a naturalization information session or citizenship ceremony, requiring only a few hours' commitment and minimal staff oversight.

Information Sessions

Information sessions take the basics of Citizenship Corners a step further through live question-and-answer sessions from knowledgeable presenters. These sessions can focus on "Know Your Rights" information presented by library staff or legal aid partners, or they can be formal USCIS information sessions led by local field officers.

"Know Your Rights" information sessions encompass simple presentations of online resources by library staff or more involved discussions of legal rights led by experts in the field. Local immigration lawyers, representatives from immigration legal aid organizations, and government immigration offices are all potential sources for "Know Your Rights" presentations or facilitators for community conversations on the topic of personal rights.

During USCIS citizenship information sessions, USCIS field officers provide immigrants and refugees with an overview of the naturalization process, describe what is required to qualify for naturalization, and distribute citizenship test preparation materials. Like a college or job fair, these information sessions make USCIS officers accessible to citizenship seekers in a more neutral, engaging environment than a government office.

The Fresno County Public Library hosts citizenship information sessions at multiple branches in the spring and fall that complement "Know Your Rights" sessions hosted by local partners. Says Michelle, "Our partnership with USCIS has been amazing. The sessions provide an overview of the naturalization process from beginning to end. Our Community Relations Officer even does a mock interview so the attendees can see firsthand what the interview might look and sound like. It allows these lawful permanent residents [to] gain a level of comfort with a very intimidating process" (Gordon 2017).

For additional information or examples, contact a library currently hosting information sessions or your local USCIS office. A list of participating libraries is available at the USCIS website: http://www.uscis.gov/citizen ship/learners/free-information-sessions.

Naturalization Ceremonies

Interestingly, due to regulations on what can and can't be part of a naturalization ceremony for new citizens, they can be even more straightforward for a library to host than information sessions. For the most part, USCIS representatives do all the work: coordinate speakers, check in participants, hand out materials (a U.S. Citizenship Welcome Packet, American flag, Citizen's Almanac, and pocket-sized versions of the Constitution and Declaration of Independence), and literally run the show. At minimum, the library involvement is simply to schedule the event and deal with the space needs (AV, seating, tables for check-in and materials, and possibly food).

According to the USCIS website, naturalization ceremonies follow a standard agenda (USCIS n.d. D):

- Play *Faces of America*, a brief USCIS video on immigration and citizenship
- Play the national anthem, "The Star-Spangled Banner"
- Welcoming remarks by the master of ceremonies
- Announce the "call of countries," a list of all the countries represented by the candidates' countries of origin
- Administer the Oath of Allegiance to the naturalization candidates
- Deliver keynote remarks (USCIS leadership or guest speaker)
- Play presidential, secretary's, or director of USCIS' congratulatory remarks
- Recite the Pledge of Allegiance
- Deliver concluding remarks (master of ceremonies or USCIS field leadership)
- Present the Certificate of Naturalization by USCIS leadership or officers (USCIS n.d.)

Some field offices offer voter registration and passport application opportunities after the ceremony; others may invite other community organizations to participate or distribute materials. You should work with the USCIS field office representatives to know exactly what they plan to do and to better accommodate their needs. Plan to provide materials about the library and its programs and services, but don't take it personally if the officers say that you can't display them during the ceremony itself; their office may have restrictions on what's allowed and what's not.

If the USCIS representatives approve, and you have kitchen space available, consider asking community members to provide snacks for the ceremony, possibly from some of the countries represented among the new citizens. More than a pleasant and welcoming addition to the ceremony itself, hosting a small reception might keep the participants in the library for a while longer, increasing the opportunity to let them know what the library has to offer. Make sure you speak with the USCIS field office representative to obtain the proper clearances when planning additional elements after the ceremony. For more on what's involved in a naturalization ceremony, visit http://www.uscis.gov/policymanual/HTML/Policy Manual-Volume12-PartJ-Chapter5.html.

Though the Fresno County Public Library is a hosting partner for larger ceremonies (200 or so participants), they have recently begun hosting much smaller ceremonies focused on younger new citizens. During what they called "the summer of citizenship," the library hosted three ceremonies for N-600s citizen applicants: youth aged 18 and under who gain citizenship automatically through a parent who is a naturalized or natural-born citizen. The ceremonies were held in the William Saroyan art gallery at the Central Library and included crafts, story time, book talks, and a world map for new citizens to mark with their country of birth. "We'll frame it and display it once it is overrun with markers," enthuses Michelle. "Our library mascot, Bentley, has also made an appearance at the ceremonies. These [smaller ceremonies] are great because the main ceremony in Fresno usually has anywhere from 500–1300 new citizens—ours are more intimate and celebratory" (Gordon 2017).

Citizenshipworks

Citizenshipworks is an online portal to completing the U.S. citizenship application, developed by the Immigration Advocates Network, the Immigration Legal Resource Center, and Pro Bono Net, supported by the Knight Foundation and the New Americans Campaign. It's different from the USCIS website in that it supports residents filling out citizenship application forms, whereas the USCIS site is where applicants keep track of their status from the moment they submit the forms.

Citizenshipworks is designed to be used directly by lawful permanent residents: prompts from the site guide them through each step of the process of filling out the citizenship application. Applicants begin by creating an account and then save their information as they add it in stages. Citizenshipworks website staff review the information along the way and let applicants know if they need to seek legal advice; if so, applicants can set up virtual appointments with Citizenshipworks legal help or be directed to organizations near them. Site-specific online help is also available.

If you can install an Internet-connected computer in or near your Citizenship Corner, visitors can use it to access the USCIS website or Citizenshipworks. Providing a dedicated computer, away from other public computers, offers applicants extra time and privacy to complete a complex application process. It removes the stress of public computer time limits and reduces the potential for others to view and steal highly sensitive personal information and identification, like passports and lawful permanent resident cards.

If your Citizenship Corner can be staffed with volunteers, they can be trained by Citizenshipworks to assist applicants with the basic navigation of the site. Accredited immigration experts working with the library can provide assistance with involved questions, either by appointment or via workshops, which we'll address in the next section.

CLASSES AND SUPPORT

Many different kinds of classes can support newcomers as they go through the process of acquiring citizenship and beginning their lives as new Americans. Your library may already offer some of these, but take a look at the full sequence of possibilities and consider which might be best for your library.

Applying for Citizenship

Information sessions provide the basics about the naturalization process, and libraries can take a more active role in supporting applicants through workshops that guide them through filling out and submitting the application itself. At the Los Angeles Public Library, librarians trained to navigate the Citizenshipworks site and application process lead classes, giving applicants a structured introduction to the platform and support while they're entering their information. Other organizations, partnered with the library, provide legal advice and guidance on immigration-related—as opposed to site-related—questions.

Citizenship workshops at the Brooklyn Public Library use a combination of online and in-person assistance. "This workshop uses interactive online interviews from Citizenshipworks.org to determine eligibility and help prepare forms," explains Eva Raison, Coordinator of Immigrant Services. "Immigration experts will be available to review applications and answer legal questions related to applying to citizenship." Registration isn't required, but those who do pre-register are given priority over drop-ins for assistance (Koerber 2016 A).

At Brooklyn's monthly workshops, participants fill out their application as a group—library staff print the completed applications at the workshops—then meet individually with a volunteer lawyer or Board of Immigration Affairs (BIA)–accredited representative from The New Americans Campaign (NAC) to review their applications. Any applicant who can answer the form's questions without needing additional help mail their own applications: if the application is complex, they're referred to NAC or another organization for more assistance (Koerber 2016 A).

Citizenship Test Preparation

After a lawful permanent resident submits their application to the government, it is reviewed and evaluated. If accepted, applicants will have two appointments scheduled: one to submit personal biometrics (fingerprints, hair/eye color, etc.) and another for the citizenship interview, which includes the official citizenship test. At the interview, the prospective new citizen answers questions about their application and personal history and then takes an oral civics test and a brief English reading and writing test; their spoken English is evaluated while they are answering the personal questions. Library-based citizenship test preparation classes can focus on all or just some of these elements.

Basic materials needed to develop a class for the civics test are available for download or purchase through the USCIS website; additional preparation materials are available from the major test prep publishers and similar sources. In a class, library staff or experienced volunteers can review the 100 questions that form the base for all citizenship civics tests and then quiz participants orally, as will happen during the interview. Although it can be helpful to go more deeply into the topics covered by the questions, don't plan on going too far unless the class discussion happens naturally. Although participants shouldn't simply memorize answers by rote, the class should stay focused on the formal questions and not introduce potentially confusing details.

The English reading and writing portions of the test ask the applicant to read a sentence—usually about United States history or civics—aloud in a way that shows they understand what they're saying and then write a spoken sentence down. An easy way to practice is to use the 100 civics and history questions as examples to read and write or other sentences from an advanced ESOL language practice book.

Finally, there's the English-speaking aspect of the citizenship interview. A dedicated interview preparation class helps in the same ways as a job interview practice session: it simulates the environment of the interview so participants are more comfortable at the real thing. Much of this portion of the interview is based on the applicant's life, so asking simple ("What is your name?") and complex ("What was the last trip you took outside the United States?") questions is a good practice. Be careful when practicing questions that would lead them to compromise sensitive information; help them review numbers and dates in general rather than asking them to recite phone numbers or birthdates.

Existing English learning programs can also easily be tailored to support those about to have their citizenship interview. Conversation groups allow English learners to practice their casual, conversational skills; basic and intermediate English classes can be targeted to focus on the questions and answers for the interview; and tutors can help applicants with areas they're struggling with. English idiom classes are also helpful, especially for local jargon and references, because it's possible that the interviewing officer might use a turn of phrase that the applicant doesn't understand, causing confusion and possibly a wrong answer.

All of these elements can be offered as separate classes, a series, or within the structure of existing programs; use the format that works best for your library and your community.

Life in the United States

Although not directly part of the citizenship process, life skills classes can be a huge benefit to new immigrants and refugees and help them answer the interview questions. In addition, like the basic services we looked at in Chapter 2, these classes can benefit anyone, including native English speakers or long-time residents.

How can life skills workshops help with citizenship? Homa Naficy of Hartford's The American Place offers this perspective: "The whole premise behind [citizenship test] questions is being changed—starting about 10–12 years ago—to make sure [applicants] really understand the values, the civic culture of America that brings us all together" (Naficy 2017). Those values are frequently expressed in how we live our daily lives in the United States, in interactions with others and the underlying reasons behind things like engaging with local government, paying taxes, and participating in a census.

Volunteer to Learn

An idea that sparked during a conversation with Homa was to offer lawful permanent residents volunteer opportunities as part of their naturalization process. Homa said, "What might help this whole naturalization process is if people contribute in community service as part of it." Volunteering at the library or at a naturalization ceremony instead of memorizing answers to civics questions could be another way to help people to get to know U.S. culture and values. She added, "If I were going to another country, I would welcome that. I'd be embarrassed to go and ask to volunteer," but if there were an established program as part of the citizenship process, "I would love that. I'd really get to know how French people are, make a friend there perhaps?" (Naficy 2017).

Many times, lessons on life skills are included as part of other programs, especially English conversation practice and job skills workshops. The advantage of a "life skills in the United States" class or series is to provide comprehensive basic information in a focused setting. Although the research for this book didn't unearth any of these programs specifically geared towards immigrants, it definitely revealed a need.

Kate Cunningham, long-time English Conversation Corner volunteer in Louisville, sees this all the time. "Learning the ropes here is difficult. [It might be helpful to have] people come and explain food stamps, health insurance, college applications and scholarships, even something about auto insurance . . . how do you explain to people from other countries that you have to have auto insurance? Or about why we pay taxes? Generally, the immigrants I've come across are very averse to paying taxes, because they've come from places with totally nonfunctional governments; they don't understand what's being taken out of their paycheck every week for unemployment insurance or workers' compensation or FICA or Medicare. That's a lot to learn and you can't learn it all at just one go around. When they first come here, the agency that's sponsoring people and brought them here may have run them by all of this in two hours. Five weeks later, when they need that information, it's not in their minds" (Cunningham 2017).

A perfect model for a newcomer-oriented "life in the United States" series is the Life Skills Academy at the San José Public Library (SJPL). In 90-minute sessions, a professional in a related field teaches teens essential life skills as they transition from high school to college, their first job, and living on their own. Teen librarians find potential speakers and work with them to develop a curriculum, presentation, and interactive activities. Topics have included "Why you shouldn't have twenty-seven credit cards" (financial literacy), "There are no potty breaks in college" (the college experience), and "Pizza is not a food group" (healthy cooking). In addition to the physical workshops, each session is recorded and posted online along with handouts and slides. Through this, says Library Director Jill Bourne, they hope to extend the reach of the program: "Our final goal is to turn each workshop into a replicable curriculum we can pass on to other libraries within the community and across the country." You can view these recordings at http://www.sjpl.org/lifeskills.

Each session averages 20 or more participants, mostly teens in the 14- to 19-year-old range. Surveys at the beginning and end of each session indicate that they are desperately needed: pre-workshop surveys report more than 75 percent of participants feeling unprepared to handle the topic, whereas post-workshop surveys drop to only 18 percent. Additional comments include suggestions for future topics, and SJPL has a growing mailing list of parents who want to be notified of each life skills program (Bourne 2017).

More stories from Kate in Louisville suggest additional topics for a "Newcomer's Guide to Living in the United States":

- **Navigating food assistance:** "It was difficult for me to learn the ropes at the food pantry [as I was helping one particular family]. You can only call between 9 and 9:30 a.m. to make an appointment for that day, and it's always busy, so you have to call again tomorrow."

- **Dealing with government agencies:** "[Another family] got a letter on Saturday saying that their passports [had] been rejected because they need to have the original of their guardianship order." They thought they'd sent it, but the helpful clerk at the post office had picked out the copy of the order, not the certified original. "So now we have to go through the whole thing again."

- **Confusing communication with officials:** "The welfare offices have to send out this notice that it's important to register to vote . . . but these people aren't citizens! If they register to vote, they're going to get in trouble! They're intimidated by the official notice: 'I didn't think I was supposed to vote, but then the letter said I was supposed to vote, but if I vote I get in trouble or get laughed out of [the polling place.]'" (Cunningham 2017) Letters like this would be a perfect topic for reading and listening comprehension exercises.

LEGAL AID

Given the increasing need for assisting lawful permanent residents on their path to citizenship, libraries are seeking better ways to provide actual legal aid to those who need it. Eva Raison at Brooklyn Public Library has a logical reason for this nontrivial step: "Libraries are historically important institutions for supporting participation in a democratic society and have served as hubs of immigrant integration across many generations. Immigration legal services seemed a good contemporary expression of that mission" (Koerber 2016 A).

One of the challenges of providing citizenship information and support is that, at some point, "help" stops being reference and becomes legal advice. As with any legal advice, it is either ill advised or actually illegal for library staff or volunteers to provide such help without the proper certification. The Southern California Association of Law Libraries (SCALL) includes a chapter on "Legal Reference vs. Legal Advice" in its publication *Locating the Law: A Handbook for Non-Law Librarians*; one section outlines what a nonattorney (aka library staff or volunteers) can and cannot do. In short, nonattorneys may recommend resources, help define legal words using a law dictionary, find relevant information via an online search, and teach research techniques. Nonattorneys may *not* recommend specific forms or explain how to fill them out (this is why Citizenshipworks requires specific training for staff or volunteers to help applicants with its site), offer opinions on handling a legal issue, interpret the law in any way, or write any legal document (including letters that applicants should be writing themselves). For more specifics, visit the SCALL website and download the chapter at http://scallnet.org/publications (Allen-Hart 2011).

Resources

A resource list, online or available in hard copy in your Citizenship Corner, is a simple way to point newcomers toward trusted and vetted immigration legal aid. If your local immigrant service offices have excellent resource lists, get hard copies to have on display and provide links to online lists via your website or research guides.

Possible resources to include are:

- Citizenshipworks
- Lists of local legal organizations/resources
- Lists of national legal resources, such as the Catholic Legal Immigration Network, Inc. (CLINIC) directory of affiliates at http://cliniclegal.org/directory
- State bar association/pro bono legal organizations, in particular, any that specialize in immigration law
- Information on avoiding immigration/citizenship scams

Immigration Scams

One of the great frustrations of helping newcomers to the United States is discovering that they have fallen victim to a criminal as they've tried to start a documented life here. On their website, USCIS describes the most common of these scams and suggests ways to help immigrants and refugees avoid them:

Scam job offers: Even before they leave their country of origin, potential immigrants to the United States receive phony job offers via email that may even ask for the person to send the "employer" money to receive their job offer!

(continued)

USCIS impersonators: Websites or individuals may impersonate official USCIS contacts and ask for money for forms, assistance, or fees. If a website asks for money to download forms or asks for an electronic funds transfer to an individual to pay for services, it's not an official USCIS contact.

"Notarios públicos": In Latin American countries, notary publics are attorneys with special credentials; in the United States, notary publics have limited roles and cannot help with immigration law. Disreputable notary publics may scam immigrants by pretending to be able to provide services they're not authorized to.

"You've won the lottery!": The U.S. State Department does maintain a Diversity Visa lottery for green card applicants, but they will never send an email to selectees.

Employer scams: Employers have received requests for I9 forms that pretend to be from USCIS, but are actually a fake email leading to a fake site. Employers of legal permanent residents or visa holders should be aware of this scam.

SOURCE: https://www.uscis.gov/avoid-scams/common-scams.

Partnerships

To extend the depth of their services to immigrants, Brooklyn Public Library works with partners like the Immigrant Justice Corps (IJC) and the New Americans Campaign (NAC) to provide legal aid. "We have a philosophy that there is no 'wrong door' for getting help, or 'wrong number.'" says Eva Raison. "Patrons start here at the library and are able to be connected to the information and service they're seeking, either within our walls or with one of our partners" (Koerber 2016 A).

The Immigrant Justice Corps launched in 2014 and sought partnerships with organizations that would able to host free immigration legal services. "We thought the library was a natural fit for the IJC program," says Eva. "We knew there was a demand for immigration legal advice, but we required the technical expertise to provide high-quality trustworthy legal consultations" (Koerber 2016 A). IJC recruits Community Fellows from law school graduates and places them with organizations serving low-income immigrants who might not be taking full advantage of available legal services, due to the barriers outlined in Chapter 1. Fellows receive training in "straightforward immigration applications such as naturalization, green card applications, and applications for Temporary Protected Status," says Victoria Nielsen, Legal Director and Interim Executive Director of the IJC (Nielsen 2017). Immigrant Justice Corps attorneys support Community Fellows with weekly supervision and assist with their accreditation with the Bureau of Immigration Appeals (BIA).

Interactions are personal and profound: a dedicated phone number to contact the library for appointments, 1:1 eligibility screenings with community fellows in private meeting rooms, application assistance, and accompaniment to the USCIS interview if needed. IJC fellows also suggest library services—job help, public benefit assistance, health insurance navigation, multilingual collections, business assistance—and referrals to other organizations the library works with. Eva offers an example: "We have relationships with a local organization that provides case management and health services to HIV+ immigrants. They're close to one of our libraries and often refer clients to IJC, but are also a support when IJC has a client who needs their services" (Koerber 2016 A).

In 2016, IJC and Brooklyn Public Library received joint funding through a two-year USCIS Citizenship and Integration Grant Program; the library will offer citizenship instruction classes at six of their most immigrant-frequented branches, and IJC will provide legal assistance to students of those classes (and others). Immigrant Justice Corps will extend their community fellows program to the Queens Public Library in the 2017–2018 fiscal year and hopes to add more libraries in the future.

Staff Certification

If you've determined there's enough demand in your community and you have staff willing to go through the process, it is possible for the library to directly offer immigration-related legal advice. The Department of Justice offers two kinds of certification to nonprofit organizations who want to provide citizenship and immigration assistance (Office of Legal Access Programs 2017):

- Accreditation for individuals: An individual is "accredited when the Office of Legal Access Programs gives permission to a specially qualified non-lawyer to represent noncitizens on behalf of a recognized organization" (they must work with a recognized organization, not on their own).
  - "Partial accreditation means representatives may go before the Department of Homeland Security (DHS) only."
  - Full accreditation means representatives may go before both DHS and the Executive Office for Immigration Review (EOIR), which includes the immigration courts and the Board of Immigration Appeals (BIA).
- "Recognition for the organization: A nonprofit, federal tax-exempt organization that has been given permission to practice immigration law through accredited representatives before the DHS (partial accreditation) or DHS and EOIR (full accreditation)."

As part of expanding their services to immigrants, both Los Angeles Public Library and Hartford Public Library have received recognition and have accredited staff. Recognition requirements for organizations include demonstrating federal tax–exempt status and that they serve primarily low-income and indigent clients, have at least one employee apply for accreditation, have access to knowledge and experience in immigration law and procedure, and designate a staff person to act as authorized officer. The paperwork for recognition can begin simultaneously with an employee applying for accreditation.

Accreditation training consists of a course provided by the Department of Justice, followed by any specialized training needed and an exam for the final accreditation. It's a long process and requires commitment on the part of staff, but it's worth it, according to Alicia Moguel, Associate Director of Lifelong Learning at Los Angeles Public Library: "We really want to work in that space because there's such a need in this city" for these services.

As of mid-2017, the Los Angeles Public Library had achieved recognition and was in the process of increasing the number of accredited staff. Alicia says, "We're in the process of determining how [these services] can work in a system as large as ours." The recognition certificate they have now is for six locations; they're beginning with services there and are potentially working towards other sites for recognition (Moguel 2017).

At Hartford, working in only one location is more straightforward, but doesn't come with an easier learning curve. After a few months of providing services, they revised their original intake process to the current model. When someone asks about citizenship help at a service desk, the staff person does a quick certification check based on the USCIS criteria (five-year residency, speaks English, over age 18, has relevant documentation). If they qualify, the applicant is given a flyer that outlines the steps to follow and documents to bring to the intake session (see the next box).

Homa Naficy of Hartford stresses the need for a two-step intake process: "In the past they came with only this document, then only that, and then they fall off the planet and show up a year later and they want their case revisited." A brief initial conversation providing instructions on the required steps, followed by a scheduled meeting with a screener who reviews their documentation and schedules an appointment with an immigration counselor, is more efficient in the long run. "That's been a much better use of the staffing skill sets and an improved process," says Homa (Naficy 2017).

Apply for U.S. Citizenship at Hartford Public Library, N-400 Screening Process

Step 1: Participate in an Intake Process at The American Place (Central Library). At intake, staff will assess your knowledge of English, provide a general overview of basic citizenship qualifications, and provide you with a detailed document checklist.

Step 2: Collect and organize ALL required documents to present to an Immigration Screener.

Step 3: Come in to meet with a Screener who will review documents during the hours listed below (no appointment necessary). M-Sa, 10-3:30, closed for lunch 12-1.

Step 4: Once YOU have collected ALL necessary documents, the Screener will make an appointment for you with a Legal Representative. The Legal Representative may need additional information or documents before reaching a decision on a client's eligibility. Upon deciding your eligibility, we anticipate completing and submitting your application within 4 weeks.

Document checklist:

- Green card
- Driver's license or state ID
- ALL passports from your country; if you can't locate older ones, bring the most recent
- Your birth certificate
- Federal tax transcripts from the past 5 years (the flyer includes information about requesting transcripts)
- A completed HPL Consultation Information Form
- If applicable, copies of any previous immigration applications and notices
- Copies of any information regarding previous citations or arrests, if applicable (the flyer includes information on getting information from the local Superior Court)

IF MARRIED, DIVORCED, AND/OR WITH CHILDREN

In addition to the above, please bring the following documents (originals or copies):

- Divorce decree(s)
- Marriage certificate(s)
- Birth certificate(s) of your children under 18
- Green card numbers of all your children and spouse

The flyer also includes information about getting the naturalization fee waived for very low-income applicants.

Technology is a key player in the success of Hartford's program; they use Cerenade's eImmigrationAIR case management system to coordinate each applicant's process. eImmigrationAIR is a web-based platform that includes a scheduling module for appointments, a robust case management system that can be configured to exactly the workflow you have, online form and client contact management tools, built-in reports, and an automatic "tracker" that searches for updates to immigration forms and procedures every night. Cerenade uses a per-user pricing model for eImmigrationAIR and offers discounts to nonprofit organizations.

Although you could use any scheduling software to coordinate your immigration services, the advantage of case management tools is in the security of your applicants' most personal information and the ability to keep all of their documents and case status in the same system. For a comparison of the four systems listed next, read this post from the American Bar Association's GPSolo magazine at http://www.americanbar.org/publi cations/gp_solo/2013/september_october/software_the_immigration _practitioner.html.

- eImmigrationAIR, http://www.cerenade.com/eimmigrationair .htm
- ImmigrationTracker, http://www.trackercorp.com/immigration -software.php
- INSZoom, http://www.inszoom.com
- LawLogix, http://www.lawlogix.com

Due to the popularity of the program in general, and especially in the political climate of 2017, Hartford is considering prioritizing low-income applicants, but initial review indicates that this includes nearly 90 percent of the newcomers who come in for services. "We're still tweaking it as we move along," says Homa (Naficy 2017).

Go Virtual

On the topic of technology, improvements in videoconferencing and online help can expand the possibilities for legal aid in libraries. As this book went to press, San José Public Library had replaced in-person sessions of their popular Lawyers in the Library program (not necessarily immigration related) with scheduled appointments in a library virtual conferencing space. Although in-person sessions might feel more personal and welcoming, virtual sessions increase the potential pool of volunteers to lawyers anywhere in the state or, possibly, the country.

San José's Lawyers in the Library program is supported by the Pro Bono Project, a local organization in Southern California dedicated to representing clients of limited means and improving access to justice (ProBonoProject n.d.). If your area has a comparable organization or network, consider approaching them with a similar idea.

SUMMING UP

The restrictions around immigration and citizenship processes in the United States can complicate the kinds of services and programs libraries want to provide to their communities, but don't let the complexity stop you. From basic Citizenship Corners, to large naturalization ceremonies, to access to legal aid, it's possible for a library of any size to support new residents as they navigate the government bureaucracy around citizenship.

A few ideas, in increasing order of straightforwardness, include:

- Provide citizenship materials and information about basic rights
- Host citizenship information sessions and naturalization ceremonies
- Offer support in the form of classes or interview practice for the citizenship process
- Help lawful permanent residents get access to legal assistance at every stage

The next chapter will offer suggestions on how libraries can support residents at any point in their naturalization process with another fundamental need: employment and workforce development.

5

◇ ◇ ◇

WORKFORCE DEVELOPMENT

From entry level to advanced, newcomers bring many skills to this country, and it's in a community's best interest to help them enter the workforce at the highest level they can. As with English language learning, libraries provide a free, neutral space for many immigrants and refugees to find the assistance they need.

Although basic job assistance in the form of résumé help and job search instruction is available at many libraries, there are special considerations to keep in mind when offering these services to immigrants and refugees. One increasingly common fact is that many newcomers arrive in the United States with advanced degrees or certifications, and the challenge is to find employment in their field. There are a growing number of resources to help newcomers in this position; we'll look at them and how libraries are involved later in this chapter.

JOB ASSISTANCE ESSENTIALS

Job assistance services at libraries usually consist of a few basic essentials:

- Lists of career-related resources, online and in the library
- Job search workshops

- Résumé help, in classes or by appointment
- Interview practice
- Computer skills classes
- Career exploration support
- College and certification test preparation materials and support
- Public technology access for typing, scanning, printing, emailing, and submitting online job applications; emailing references; and acquiring transcripts online

Some libraries also have dedicated staff to provide individualized help or programs for people to returning to the workforce later in life or after incarceration, but these tend to be add-ons to the core services mentioned earlier. Even without being tailored to newcomers, these basics serve them effectively when applied with the accessibility addressed in Chapter 2.

If your library already has strong programs in job assistance, language learning, and citizenship, congratulations! You're providing an excellent service to newcomer residents, and the remainder of this chapter will give you examples of how to adapt your services to their specific needs.

If you're looking for ways to improve your existing workforce development services that will include newcomers easily, consider these changes:

- Offer job search, résumé, and computer skills workshops in your community's high-impact languages as well as English.
- Incorporate résumé writing and cover letter practice into existing ESOL programs (work-specific ESOL programs are covered later in this chapter).
- If your city or state has an expanded municipal ID program or is following in California's footsteps and providing a nonidentification/driving-purposes-only license, display information on how to apply for these documents.

There are many examples of comprehensive career and job centers at libraries across the country; the following are a few to look at:

The Cuyahoga Works Job and Career Services Department at the Cuyahoga (OH) County Public Library was created in 1976 and "offers career counseling, single-topic workshops, a 15-week Job Seekers series, and programs for teens and seniors. Cuyahoga Works has four credentialed Rehabilitation Counselors on staff" who oversee personality, skill, interest, and values assessments and give individual assistance as needed (Koerber 2016 C).

Los Angeles Public Library has a WorkSource Center Portal at the Central Library that arranges 1:1 assistance for job seekers in finding and securing a job, writing résumés, sharpening interview skills, and considering new professions. WorkSource programs are also offered at multiple branch locations (Los Angeles Public Library n.d.).

In Rhode Island, the Rhode Island ALLAccess (ALL stands for Adult Lifelong Learning) program was designed to give libraries a platform to innovate and integrate adult education and workforce services serving all adults, with an emphasis on adults with low levels of digital or English literacy, low education attainment, or disabilities. ALLAccess services include drop-in Learning Lounges; "Clubs" for technology, typing, and jobs support; assistive technology stations; and similar services (ALLAccess RI n.d.).

Even a single event can be multipurpose if marketed to specific audiences. For a while, the Ocotillo Workforce & Literacy Center at the Phoenix (AZ) Public Library hosted Recruitment Thursdays, "lunchtime drop-in programs where large companies and small businesses networked with potential employees in a less-formal environment" (Koerber 2016 C). Coupled with the immigrant-focused services to entrepreneurs discussed later in this chapter, an event like Recruitment Thursdays becomes an even richer networking opportunity for all.

The Free Library of Philadelphia chose to help create a network of community organizations to increase basic job assistance services to immigrants in the highly diverse Southwest Philadelphia neighborhood surrounding the library's Paschalville branch. The Paschalville Partnership is a coalition of 11 organizations committed to raising local employment levels by training their staff to provide additional services, coordinating between partnerships to extend services, and implementing proactive communication between the community and the organizations. The initiative focused on increasing the number and accessibility of literacy and ESL courses, job-skills training, computer access and skills training, and additional services as necessary. The city had deemed the area a "service desert," where the needs of the residents were far greater than services available, and supported the development of the Paschalville Partnership to provide an oasis. The library chose to become a backbone organization for this effort due to anecdotal evidence from Paschalville Library staff members, who daily encountered residents with barriers to employment well beyond the typical job seeker (Kallenbach & Nash 2016).

In a 2017 Institute for Museum and Library Services (IMLS) blog post, Annette Mattei, project coordinator for the Partnership at the library, sums up the reasoning: "If a catalyst causes or accelerates a reaction without itself being affected, then I would agree that libraries are in the perfect position to act as *community* catalysts. That has certainly been my observation, serving as project coordinator" (Mattei 2017).

By the first full year of implementation, the partnership had created two Job Readiness Labs (JRLs) at the Paschalville Library and at the Southwest CDC (Community Development Corporation) location. JRLs provide free computer and Internet access and 1:1 assistance by walk-in or by appointment for creating or updating résumés, setting up email and other online accounts, conducting Internet searches, and applying for jobs online. Weekly workshops, bimonthly employment "boot camps," and quarterly community open houses give job seekers opportunities to hone soft skills (workplace etiquette, businesslike conduct, appropriate attire, etc.) and practice networking skills in low-stakes environments.

JRL staff will also refer job seekers with specific needs to partner organizations for focused help; immigrants and refugees are as likely, if not more likely, to have these needs than U.S.-born residents. Adults who have been out of work for a long time or are looking to switch career paths are directed to the PA CareerLink system; adults functioning below basic education levels or who need to brush up on their skills are referred to adult education evaluation at the Southwest CDC and then are referred to local adult basic education (ABE) providers. Residents dealing with financial issues that impede a job search—such as debilitating debt, default payments and judgments, or poor credit ratings—are set up with free counseling and workshops offered through the city's Financial Empowerment Center.

One story provided by the Paschalville branch describes a typical JRL experience: "A man from Liberia needed assistance filling out online applications as well as setting up an email [account]. He had been coming in each week to receive help and instruction. After being interviewed and offered a conditional offer of employment, he came back to our lab for further assistance with completing prerequisite online training and child abuse clearance to start his new position" (Mattei 2016).

Although most job assistance programs are directed at adults, teens who are already working or about to begin their work life need help, too. In May 2016, the Rhode Island Family Literacy Initiative (RIFLI) became the backbone organization for an IMLS grant project to develop youth-driven and -centered, competency-based programming that will create and promote workforce development opportunities for teens. The project encourages innovative programs and hopes to develop frameworks driven by student interests and aligned with education and workforce standards.

WORK-SPECIFIC LANGUAGE HELP

In addition to the ESOL learning opportunities discussed in the previous chapter, libraries offer diverse types of language programs geared toward the workplace. In this section, you'll explore accent reduction and pronunciation workshops, interview practice, profession-specific ESOL classes, and driver's education classes.

Accent Reduction and Pronunciation

While new English speakers are first gaining proficiency, critiquing their pronunciation might undermine their confidence in learning. In a dedicated accent reduction or pronunciation class, the goal is to work with individuals who already know some basic English so that they can learn how English sounds are made, refining the knowledge they already have.

Pronunciation practice is an essential part of job assistance because, unfortunately, speaking heavily accented English can be a barrier to employment or promotion. From food service to leading neighborhood development meetings, speaking clearly to be understood is vital for any position that requires interacting with the general public and is an asset for career growth.

As mentioned in Chapter 3, pronunciation workshops zero in on the sounds of spoken English and how regional accents affect them. Workplace-related pronunciation practice could focus on a particular industry or topic, practice customer service interactions, or involve interview preparation sessions; the point is to give each participant an opportunity to practice shaping the sounds that aren't familiar to them and striving for clarity.

Interview Preparation

Interview preparation and practice designed for newcomers begins with the typical structure—role playing as interviewer and interviewee to develop comfort in asking and answering questions and getting feedback on responses—and then goes further. Additional topics could include learning and practicing workplace terminology and jargon, discussing how U.S. workplaces may differ in culture and norms from their country of origin, and question-and-answer practice.

<table>
<tr><td>

Say It Again, Differently

As non-English speakers work to add to their vocabulary, one challenge is rephrasing what they've said if the listener doesn't seem to understand them. Offering a nonjudgmental, supportive space for English learners to practice repeating the same information using different words—that they may speak more clearly or are more locally well known—would be especially useful for job applicants.

</td></tr>
</table>

Interview preparation help can work as a 1:1, small group, or large group program. On an individual or small group level, participants get more opportunities to practice answering typical interview questions, are able to ask their own questions of the leader or group, and can receive related advice such as what to wear or how early to be for the interview. In a larger group, you can reach more people at once, but it will tend to be more general unless you can break out the participants into smaller interest groups after a main presentation.

Profession-Specific ESOL Classes

As evidenced by the large numbers of profession-specific language dictionaries, many terms and phrases need specific translation within different fields. Some may be direct translations—for example, disinfectant is el desinfectante in Spanish—but others are more colloquial, especially if the language is structured differently than English. Although it's not absolutely necessary to have native speakers or professional translators of the target languages offer these programs, it may help with those more indirect translations and with answering related questions from participants.

Medical terminology and customer service language are two popular topics to focus an ESOL class on, because of the highly technical nature of the former and the universality of the latter. For medical terminology, one approach is to find a local nursing or physician's assistant program with a high percentage of non-native English speakers among their students. Alternatively, look for a community health organization that works with local immigrant or refugee populations and ask them if they'd be willing to lead or develop sessions on the most needed terms for careers in medical records, healthcare, or related fields. This could be a part of a larger series on health language for daily life or part of a workforce development plan.

The basic language of customer service is useful in nearly every job, whether people are dealing with the public or providing services to other people in their company. If you're a native English speaker with no other languages developing a program, use a book like *Outreach Spanish* by William C. Harvey to compile a list of basic words and phrases to include; this book teaches English speakers the Spanish equivalents, but the table of contents can be a start for brainstorming class content. Although it's less necessary to find a native speaker to help with translation, you could also seek out a local business owner or human resources representative who is a native speaker of the target language to facilitate questions.

Later in this chapter you'll learn about a new program at the Hartford Public Library that includes ESOL classes for the food service industry.

Driver's Education Classes

Driver's education is included in this chapter because it might be an important part of daily life—frequently, people need to drive to work. Once again, your community needs should drive a push to offer this kind of program; younger immigrants will (probably) get driver's education through school, and people resettling to the United States in large towns or cities may not need to drive for their daily life. That said, for adult newcomers in or outside of cities who are seeking employment, driving radically increases the range within which they can look, and a valid driver's license is a requirement for many jobs.

It is crucial for drivers in the United States to know how to read road signs and emergency information signs in English, but offering driving-related classes in languages other than English can facilitate a more thorough understanding of the rules of the road, leading to safer drivers on the streets. At their most basic, driver's education classes for immigrants can be similar to the profession-specific ESOL classes and focus on learning the English words for terms they may know in another language.

In the past, RIFLI has offered an ESOL-specific driver's education class at Providence-area libraries. "The driver's ed class is for ESL learners who want help prepping for the written test," explained Karisa Tashjian, Director of RIFLI. "We discuss driving laws, review basic signs, and spend a lot of time practicing vocabulary." She was quick to add, "We don't do the on-the-road practice, though" (Koerber 2016 A). If you can partner with a local high school or driving school to offer these classes, it can make offering them more straightforward and would work within local restrictions on who can and can't lead a driver's ed class. If not, try starting with a vocabulary class, and perhaps you can scale up to teaching the rules of the road in a future program.

EDUCATION AND TRAINING RESOURCES

One of the reasons libraries are so well positioned to offer workforce development programs is that what is offered is usually free and open to anyone in the community. For those who are currently out of work and need to learn skills or get retraining to enter a new field, this can make the difference between being limited to below-minimum-wage work and entering a field in which they might be able to advance a career.

Library workforce development programs can particularly serve immigrants and refugees because these residents may not have any other affiliations, such as an existing workplace or school, that would offer them training. Private skill-building classes often charge significant fees, and continuing education programs can be expensive, limited to existing students/professionals, or both.

KentuckianaWorks, the Louisville workforce development investment board, analyzed Louisville's economic growth and determined that many potential applicants lacked the coding skills needed to succeed in the blossoming technology industry. In 2013, KentuckianaWorks and the Louisville Free Public Library launched CodeLouisville, a program that pairs coding learners with IT professional mentors. The library provides computer time and the learning platforms Treehouse and Lynda.com for CodeLouisville participants with library cards; CodeLouisville staff do the matchmaking between learners and mentors, and provide participants with additional support (Chant 2015).

In Nevada, the need for prospective employees to update existing manufacturing skills to work at companies like Tesla inspired a more comprehensive training effort. Nevada Working Capital (NWC), a partnership between the Carson City Library (CCL) and Western Nevada College (WCN), brought an entirely new kind of training and certification process into a public library: manufacturing technician. "Participants had training options based on their time and education needs," explains Diane Baker, Business Management Director and NWC Project Manager. For certification applicants, the library offered "fast track, super-fast-track, and self-paced" programs, and the college offered semester-based classes; the partnership also provided additional classes on SolidWorks (specialized engineering software), presentation skills, and computer skills. "Grant funds paid for the certification test fees. During the 1-year pilot, CCL and WCN helped 64 students ages 18 and older earn the Manufacturing Technician 1 (MT1) certification; currently CCL offers the self-paced training program and periodic proctored exams, and is pursuing options for partial fee scholarships. CCL has also shared what they've learned about

providing MT1 certification with a nearby Nevada library system" (Koerber 2016 C).

In contrast, a new program coordinated by the Hartford Public Library
is designed specifically for non-English speakers. The Career Pathways
pilot project is oriented around the food service and hospitality industry,
because it's an industry that is growing rapidly nationally and one that
many immigrants are already involved in.

Career Pathways has three components structured to help job seekers at
varying levels of skill and literacy. Immigrants with a lower English literacy and work skills level attend dedicated ESOL classes to learn the language they need for entry-level work in a kitchen. The goal, however, goes
far beyond dishwashing: the program centers on institutional food service, such as in schools, senior centers, and hospitals, a career path that can
lead to long-term, benefitted positions at the management level.

Complementing the ESOL classes, the library helps participants find
placement at kitchens in Hartford-area public schools. Homa Naficy of
Hartford describes the reasoning behind this connection: "We partnered
with the Hartford Public Schools (HPS) Food & Children's Nutrition Services because they are the biggest production kitchens of food service
delivery in Hartford. I think libraries don't understand the power of these
full kitchens. HPS has 53 kitchens and they're always looking to build staff
capacity there, so it's been a win-win situation all around" (Naficy 2017).

In the second component, Career Pathways encourages and offers support to current immigrant employees in the industry to study for and take
their SERV-SAFE certification exam. Most states require at least some
training in food safety for employees, and many require official SERV-
SAFE certification by at least some employees at any establishment. Hartford provides computer time and learning skills assistance to participants
as they work through online training materials provided by SERV-SAFE,
helping them dramatically increase their career options and earning
potential as food service workers and managers.

Finally, a third element of the program recognizes that many immigrant
workers—and their employers—are unaware of their rights as employees.
Library trainings include education on what rights employees in Connecticut have and how to assert them in the workplace. An undercurrent of
the initiative is to also educate employers about the employee rights of the
immigrants they hire.

Career Pathways has already seen success, says Homa. "The program
started just about a year ago and they've hired 17 people at the HPS kitchens. It's working, and it fits with what we do at the library." Future plans
include restructuring the program to accommodate more participants and

doing active outreach to find them, expanding to include other fields, and perhaps cultural exchanges of food amongst participants (Naficy 2017).

SUPPORT PROFESSIONALS AND ENTREPRENEURS

An increasing need among newcomers is support in continuing the careers that have been interrupted by travel to the United States, especially in the case of refugees fleeing political disturbance and violence in their home countries. In a 2016 report, the Migration Policy Institute (MPI) states that 25 percent of college-educated immigrants in the United States either cannot find jobs or are employed in low-skilled work. In contrast, this "brain waste" was estimated to affect 18 percent of college-educated U.S.-born residents. MPI estimates that not employing these immigrants at their full potential costs the United States nearly $40 billion each year in forgone earnings (money they could be making in professional positions) and more than $10 billion in forgone taxes on those earnings (Batalova, Fix, & Bachmeier 2016).

Professional Credentialing

The single biggest challenge for these highly educated immigrants is convincing employers or credentialing organizations to recognize and honor out-of-country degrees and certifications without significant effort and expense. Magnifying the problem is the reality that these immigrants frequently need to work lower-paying jobs while they're trying to recredential and may be supporting families as well.

Supporting these professionals can be as simple as a bit of special attention. The chapter on English language learning referred to Bill, a helper at Louisville's English Conversation Clubs, and a physician he worked with. Kate Cunningham, senior helper at the ECC, tells the story: "Bill was working assiduously, every Saturday, with a young physician from Asia who needed to improve his spoken English for the patient examination routine," a mock patient interview that is part of the U.S. Medical Licensing Examination required to work in the medical field. "The young man from Asia was able to pass that test, and we were so happy to get a new physician, though I think he left Louisville afterwards. Another friend of mine worked with a young physician from Cuba who was very bright, spoke very fast English," but needed to work on enunciation. "[Several volunteers] worked with Maria to get her to clip her English so she could go up to Chicago, do the interview, and become a practicing pediatrician . . .

These are two physicians that I know of, and I think there have probably been a couple more that needed a little extra personal help to speak more slowly and clearly, and were motivated to become practicing physicians. We rejoice in those success stories" (Cunningham 2017).

Sophie Maier, head of the ECC program at Louisville, gives another example: "One of our big success stories came to both the ECC and was also one of the co-founders of our Spanish literary salon. He was a professor, the head of the Spanish department at a university in Cuba. When he got here, he was cleaning toilets, working three different jobs, working on his English when time allows." He came to the library with the idea for a Spanish literary salon to demonstrate how his skills could benefit his new community. During the salons, he connected with university students and professors who were attending as participants, and they were able to help him get into a master's in Spanish program at a school in Louisville." (Yes, a native Spanish speaker was required to get an advanced degree in *Spanish* to be able to teach.) Sophie adds, "Now he's an adjunct professor at a private university, and just suffers the indignities of any adjunct professor. He still has a job as a hospital aide, but at least he's at a university and having an impact on students' lives" (Maier 2017).

Two libraries who participated in the Networks for Integrating New Americans project (see Chapter 1 for more information) took different approaches to helping immigrants with advanced credentials reignite their career in the United States.

As part of the ALLAccess program in Rhode Island, RIFLI director Karisa Tashjian worked with the We Rhode Island Network (WeRIN) to build job readiness, digital literacy, and English language skills. ALLAccess programs largely consist of drop-in Learning Lounges and technology help; participants in the Jobs Clubs visit local employers for workplace tours and the opportunity to ask questions of human resources staff and receive referrals for additional training. Says Tashjian, "We try to raise employer awareness with personal outreach and a brochure highlighting WeRIN's high-quality educational services and promoting the outstanding job candidates we work with" (Koerber 2016 A).

In Boise, Global Talent Idaho (GTI)—initially supported by Neighbors United, an immigrant services network that includes the Boise Public Library and now a self-sustaining organization—"was started in 2014 to address the individual and systemic barriers to employment that well-educated and highly skilled immigrants and refugees face." Through formal training and personalized coaching, GTI has helped more than 100 job seekers resume their professional careers in the United States (Global Talent Idaho n.d. A); via their website, GTI also educates potential employers on how GTI-vetted candidates can become contributing employees and makes connections through online resumes posted by candidates (Global Talent Idaho n.d. B).

If you want to go beyond the direct connection making of the kind RIFLI provides through ALLAccess, consider partnering with an organization like Global Talent Idaho to provide additional services to immigrants and refugees with advanced degrees or professional credentials in your area. Some groups include:

- Global Talent Idaho, http://globaltalentidaho.org.
- Upwardly Global, a national organization that creates partnerships with employers to place college-educated immigrants and provides customized training and support to job seekers, http://www.upwardlyglobal.org.
- "NACES is an association of independent, nongovernmental organizations providing credential evaluation services to individuals who have completed part or all of their education outside the United States" (NACES n.d.). NACES members will evaluate a newcomer's education or professional credentials and help them choose next steps, http://www.naces.org.

Support Entrepreneurs

A recent trend in libraries is finding ways to support small business owners and entrepreneurs in our community. One path to success for many immigrants is to start their own business, from mobile app development to yogurt: the founder and CEO of Chobani, Hamdi Ulukaya, immigrated from Turkey and got his start selling homemade feta cheese.

Sometimes, exposure is the best thing a library can offer to a new business owner. Sarah Kelley-Chase, formerly of the Hillcrest location of the Boise Public Library, describes an unexpected outcome of a cultural sharing program: "There was a gentleman—Kibrom—who was starting a restaurant at the time, an Eritrean restaurant, so he brought in food. He actually has a free-standing, well-run amazing restaurant now not too far from downtown" (Kelley-Chase 2017). (You'll learn more about the Worlds Connect programs at Boise in Chapter 6.)

Supporting entrepreneurs is another opportunity for existing library programs to serve newcomer populations, with small changes to accommodate diverse English literacy skills. At the Buffalo & Erie County Public Library, the Career Center offers small business workshops in strategic planning and marketing and hosts daylong workshops with partner organ-izations covering legal issues, insurance, business finance, and similar topics. Databases such as Morningstar Investment Research Center, Demo-graphics Now: Business & People, and several Gale/Cengage collections provide authoritative data useful to small businesses. However, Director Mary Jean Jakubowski says the library is looking to expand the program, "bringing workshops to offsite locations and working more actively with local organizations instrumental in helping immigrants start their own small businesses. As their staff becomes more knowledgeable of the ser-vices and resources available for free at the Library, they have increasingly referred their clients to our 37 branches" (Jakubowski 2017).

For other areas, a larger and more organized approach can have a sig-nificant impact. According to the Department of Small Business Services (SBS), "nearly half of New York City's 220,000 businesses are owned by immigrants" (Torres-Springer & Agarwal n.d.). Responding to that fact, SBS developed an Immigrant Business Initiative in 2014 to fund innova-tive service models that provide entrepreneurs with the resources they need to succeed. "Supporting immigrant entrepreneurs is vital to support-ing the growth of New York City's economy," said Gregg Bishop, Com-missioner of SBS (Koerber 2016 C).

The initiative provides funding based on the language group of the tar-get audience, so in 2015, the Brooklyn Public Library used funding to expand their popular English language PowerUP! Business Plan Compe-tition to Brooklyn's Haitian and Kreyol-speaking community. Eva Raison, Coordinator of Immigrant Services at Brooklyn, explained that choice: "Haiti is the most common country of origin in our ESOL and Citizenship programs, and we had a strong relationship with several Caribbean busi-ness assistance nonprofits" (Koerber 2016 C). [After three years, Brooklyn Public Library no longer offers the program; Kreyol speakers are encour-aged to participate in the all-language PowerUP! Competition, with lan-guage assistance provided by the library.]

Potential participants in PowerUP! Kreyol attended an orientation ses-sion at a local library conducted in English, Haitian Kreyol, and French. Applicants then participated in free bilingual (Kreyol/English) classes, such as Business Plan, Marketing Plan, Financial Projections, or Library Resources, and met with a business counselor through the program's partner, the Haitian American Business Assistance Center. The Business Library's outreach specialist and a part-time program coordinator—who are bilingual in Kreyol—were available to assist participants with research and support as they developed their plans. Participants submitted their business plans and presented before a panel of judges to determine the top three proposals, with prizes ranging from $2,000 (third place) to $5,000 (first place) awarded at a public ceremony.

In 2015, as an extension of the initiative, the SBS approached the New York, Queens, and Brooklyn public libraries to offer free business courses in the top six languages spoken in New York City. Explains Eva, "SBS hires instructors and schedules classes with the library in neighborhoods where we serve large communities of the target language group" (Koerber 2016 C), including Spanish, Russian, Chinese, Kreyol, and Arabic. The library also provides marketing for the initiative: courses are posted on the BPL [Brooklyn Public Library] website and multilingual flyers about SBS are included in New American Corners in every BPL branch (Koerber 2016 C).

SUMMING UP

There are many overlaps between the employment needs of immigrants and long-term residents, and a robust library workforce development program can serve all of these needs very well. Some of the special circumstances around newcomers to the United States can lead to additional programs that address these needs as well:

- Basic and workplace-specific English language learning programs
- Accent reduction and pronunciation practice
- Interview preparation with a focus on clear speech
- Driver's education classes (no driving practice!)
- Targeted assistance to specific local industries/fields and entrepreneurs
- Help for newly arrived professionals to transfer their credentials to U.S. organizations

This chapter is the last that focuses strictly on the integration aspects of improved services to immigrants and other newcomers. Chapter 6 will add in the celebratory ways that receiving communities can show their welcome to their new residents, and those new residents can introduce their neighbors to the rich culture and traditions they bring with them.

6
◆ ◆ ◆

CULTURAL PROGRAMS

In Chapter 1, you learned about the three pillars of immigrant integration: language, civic, and economic. Whereas the other chapters in this book are clear fits with individual pillars, cultural programs can address all three and go beyond them. As such, cultural programs developed around newcomer audiences, presenters, or both can achieve many goals:

- Serves non-English speakers in their native languages
- Celebrates the nonlocal cultures of new arrivals
- Gives everyone an opportunity to share their cultural heritage and learn about others
- Provides opportunities for questions and discussions between people of varied backgrounds
- Increases the world knowledge of local-born residents
- Gives people learning languages other than English a chance to practice
- Increases the diversity of literary and more traditional library programs (film series, story times, etc.)

SHARING PROGRAMS

Cultural sharing programs are exactly that: opportunities for new residents (or not-so-new) in a community to share the culture, stories, foods, music, dance, and life of their place of origin with their neighbors. In this section, you'll look at different styles of programs; in the next section, programs and events focused on specific topics or themes will be addressed.

A note on religion and culture: although much of American culture is secular—despite or due to the many religions represented here—the same is not necessarily true in other countries. What they consider cultural may include clearly religious images and themes; art from Spanish-speaking countries is a common example of this overlap, but the blend of culture and religions happens all around the world. As neutral spaces, libraries must be aware of and respectful of this fact and prepare for the questions and concerns that might arise from showcasing this work. In some cases, these programs might be an opportunity to reframe conversations in the community about the intersection of culture and religion.

Similarly, food is often an important element of a person's culture. If your library has existing limits on when and how food can be included in programs, make sure to plan with these restrictions in mind and communicate them clearly to participating community members. Again, be respectful of what certain foods mean to them culturally, and make sure to emphasize that these limits are for every program, including ones run entirely by the library. Alternatively, if your library has been considering changing these restrictions, cultural sharing programs may be a catalyst to do so, especially if you have buy-in from library or city/county administration or the library Friends group.

Exhibitions and Displays

Displays are a very basic type of library program and are often one of the most effective. Creating book displays or hosting exhibitions of art or 3D objects are second nature to library staff, and the displays can be used occasionally or regularly to highlight the cultures arriving along with waves of immigrants and refugees.

Consider featuring your book displays prominently near the front of the library; age-targeted in the children's, teen, or adult spaces; or permanently hosted next to Citizenship Corners if space permits. They can be part of national efforts—black and Latinx (a gender-neutral variant of Latino/a) history months, winter or spring holiday displays, Welcoming Week in September—or inspired by shifts in local demographics. Monthly exhibits can engender excitement, whereas longer-lived or permanent displays become a resource that visitors return to regularly.

Displays of library materials could be geared to all ages or narrowed down to children, teens, or adults and might include:

- Nonfiction titles about countries of origin, including materials on religion, history, and different aspects of the culture
- Fiction titles set in that country written by native authors or featuring characters from those places who have relocated/immigration stories
- Information about the different peoples from the country of origin, especially if there are multiple significant cultural differences
- Poetry, plays, or other literature from a country
- Documentaries or feature films on or set in a country
- Music or other audio from that country
- Cookbooks or other home-based skills from those countries

Another possibility is to invite artists, writers, or other creators from immigrant or refugee communities to contribute to a locally focused display or exhibition. Again, this can be a permanent or rotating collection, depending on need and space. A tremendous diversity of artistic style is arriving daily from countries around the world, and it's possible to showcase folk art with ancient imagery next to contemporary art made of modern materials and writing from personal stories along with rewritten mythologies.

To look for established creators, talk to local immigrant or refugee organizations or the folks who are already visiting the library. Ask if they are or know anyone who might be looking for a place to display their works, and be sure to convey that you are not concerned about them being "professional" artists or writers. As you engage in outreach with agencies serving immigrant and refugee populations, frequently mention that the display and exhibition spaces at the library are available to host shows curated by these organizations.

Of course, you could also host a program to provide opportunities for creation as well. From story time crafts to creative writing workshops, anything goes. If you already have a local-author, self-publishing, or creative writing series, try marketing your program specifically to immigrants and refugees to encourage them to share their stories. Cultural showcases (discussed in the next section) could include an art-making session, and any art-focused creative programs could occasionally be held in other languages to encourage participation by those populations. Whatever you're already doing, determine if it's something that can be reimagined or tweaked slightly to be more open to contributions from immigrant or refugee participants.

Another approach comes from actively partnering with a community organization already serving these populations to showcase work done by their constituents or clients. This is an especially effective way to work with family literacy or community learning organizations that have a steady stream of creativity coming from children and their caregivers. Schools, out-of-school care programs, daycares, and similar places provide other ready-made streams of work, as do communities built around mosques, temples, churches, and other places of worship.

Cultural Showcases

A more dynamic way to share cultures of newcomers is through library-hosted cultural showcases. Whereas a display or exhibition is largely static, a showcase event brings together members of immigrant or refugee communities with the local-born residents to share food, music, dance, clothing, stories, and much more. Again, these might be regularly scheduled or done as new waves of immigrants come to the area; each showcase might be a two-hour program or an all-day event, whatever works for an individual library.

Cultural showcases are an excellent way to invite members of a cultural community to share with others what's important to them. Some might bring clothing and home textiles to display on a table; others can share library-friendly food and drink. There could be performances of dance or music, or an opportunity for everyone to learn to sing, dance, or play a particular piece. Alternatively, music might be playing softly in the background for the entire event via recordings or by live performers.

Rather than a lecture (discussed later), this is a chance for everyday members of the community to participate and contribute personal aspects of their culture to share with their new neighbors. Stories and jokes can be shared while children engage in crafts or free play. Daily life is the focus, rather than an academic discussion.

Although it's possible to hold a cultural showcase in conjunction with a holiday from that culture, it's not required; special occasions often deserve their own celebration, separate from an opportunity to learn about a culture as a whole.

After the English Conversation Clubs mentioned in Chapter 3, some of the most popular programs at the Iroquois Branch of the Louisville Free Public Library are the Cultural Showcases. Sophie Maier was inspired to initiate this series by watching interactions during the Conversation Clubs. "Having seen folks in intense conversations and cultural exchanges during the English Conversation Club, including sharing of photos and even music, I saw there was a demand for programming that would allow folks to share their culture with more time and a bigger 'stage.' I started with spotlighting some newly arrived populations and then began to include groups that had been around much longer, including one for Native Americans" (Maier 2017).

Showcases are typically held on the third Saturday of the month, just before the English Conversation Club session, and might include snacks, live music, dance, games, decorations, and sometimes a PowerPoint presentation. Sophie asks participants to highlight positive, inclusive aspects of their culture, but it's not always easy: "Many of our families are refugees from war, and we as a city resettle folks from 'all sides,' as it were. That was probably one of the biggest challenges from the onset. I wanted to make clear that everyone was welcome and that the emphasis was on the positive and agreed-upon beauty of any given culture."

Audiences are as diverse as participants, coming from a neighborhood where more than 100 languages are spoken. Sophie says, "Those who had recently moved from a more homogenous country get to learn about folks from all over the world, but more importantly, they have the chance to truly hear the stories of their new neighbors, classmates, and workmates. Breaking bread together and dancing to music is very uniting!" In the beginning, Sophie organized a Cultural Showcase every month, but has decreased the frequency due to the work involved; she's trying to inspire other Louisville locations to hold Showcases, as well as spread the word about the English Conversation Corners (Maier 2017).

Shortly after the Boise Public Library's Hillcrest location opened, staff responded to the influx of refugees in nearby apartment buildings by creating the Worlds Connect Program, a similar concept to Louisville's Cultural Showcases. Sarah Kelley-Chase, former branch manager at Hillcrest, explains: "Worlds Connect was an effort on the part of staff to help families that were moving in get to know the library and their new neighbors and vice versa, the existing neighbors would get to know the new residents." Unlike the Cultural Showcases, Worlds Connect has always been a periodic series, with a new program developed as another wave of newcomers arrives from a different area of the world. "It varies," says Sarah. "Some years we have lots of new folks in and some years we don't have quite as many. It's been going for something like 8–9 years." Currently, there isn't a single point person in charge of the series, and Worlds Connect programs are now developed on an ad hoc basis.

Though irregular, the format is roughly the same for each Worlds Connect event: a participant talks about their experiences or what their life was like in their country, what the transition has been like here, or what their profession was or their passion; other elements of the culture may be displayed through food, music, information, or decorations.

For Sarah, one of the most memorable Worlds Connect programs centered on Eritrean refugees. "We had a couple of people bring in slides and tell their stories. We had someone come in and do a coffee ceremony, which made the library smell absolutely amazing!" Another participant was Kibrom, the entrepreneur mentioned in Chapter 5. He brought samples of Eritrean cuisine as snacks for the program and to promote his new restaurant downtown. Adds Sarah, "Worlds Connect was part of getting the word out for [the restaurant], which was awesome in that we had someone come in and make a go of it and be successful" based on word of mouth and exposure at the program (Kelley-Chase 2017).

Craft Programs

Whether presented as part of another program or on their own, crafts can be a meaningful, enlightening, and enjoyable way to share details of a culture.

Many countries have unique or exemplary patterns or styles of knitting, crochet, embroidery, appliqué, or other embellishments; or have wardrobe elements that can be created during a single session (scarves, hair adornments, jewelry, etc.). When the objective isn't just another craft program but a focus on cultural sharing and education, the discussion around the cultural significance of the work becomes as important as learning the craft itself, and this fact should be emphasized to participants. (Whether they listen or not is up to them, of course.)

If your library already offers a knitting/crochet group or a sewing circle, approach the attendees and see if they might be interested in participating in a more culturally focused session. If you know of groups of crafters who already exist in immigrant or refugee communities, offer them space in the library and see if they'd be willing to teach a workshop. Use your outreach contacts (discussed in the next chapter) to find additional resources for learners and presenters, as well as for marketing the program once you've put it together.

Like textile arts, paper arts are nearly universal due to an inexpensive and short materials list, usually just paper and scissors or straight blades. There are strong paper arts traditions throughout the world to explore for programs:

- European paper cutting:
  - German and Swiss *scherenschnitte*
  - Eastern European decorative cutting, using black or brightly colored paper: *vycinanka* (Belarus), *wycinanki* (Poland), *vytynanky* (Ukraine)
  - Silhouette cutting from Eastern and Central Europe
  - Jewish diaspora decorative paper cutting
- *Papel picado* from Mexico
- *Sanjhi* paper cutting in India, often used as patterns for colored sand, rice, and flower Rangoli art
- Chinese *jianzhi* paper cutting
- Japanese *origami* (paper folding) and *kirigami* (paper cutting)
- Indonesian *batik* (fabric dyeing) can also be done to paper, then used for folding or cutting
- And, of course, holiday-related paper crafts and paper planes

Many books are available that illustrate modern paper cutting styles with ancient cultural motifs, but many paper cutting traditions themselves go back hundreds or thousands of years. If it's possible to find paper cutters among your immigrant populations, encourage them to come and demonstrate their art; if not, how-tos and books are available on most of these traditions, and the techniques are simple to learn.

The extra magic of a handcraft-based program is that it can provide the ease needed for speakers of multiple languages to participate, even if the program itself isn't labeled as being for English learners or newcomers. "Coloring Anonymous (CA)" is a series at the Cedar Falls (IA) Public Library inspired by the current craze in adult coloring books; the library provides materials and a space for quiet but interactive coloring for anyone who wants to sit down and join. Erin Thompson, Technology Librarian and facilitator of CA, noticed an interesting change over the first few months of the program. "I don't have specifics on race, ethnicity, or citizen status (I don't like to make assumptions), but I've noticed an increase in diversity as the program progressed, based on the languages spoken by the attendees. In the beginning, it was only English, but recently I've heard four separate languages during a program—Spanish, Arabic, Hindi, and English—among about 15 attendees."

Curious, Erin spoke with one participant about how she'd heard of Coloring Anonymous; Cedar Falls is trying to increase services to underserved patrons, including newcomers, all speakers of other languages, homeless persons, and other marginalized groups. "She said her friend told her about the program, so I know word is getting out and we are hopeful to reach even more people." When asked why a general-interest program like Coloring Anonymous might appeal to such a diverse audience, Erin answers, "My personal theory is that it is a safe, welcoming program featuring a 'language' that is universal—art. We invite all ages and it is a free program with all supplies provided, so families often color together." The program certainly attracts fans: Erin estimates that 75 percent of participants repeatedly attend the program, though new people start up all the time (Thompson 2017).

Taking the crafts idea a step further, the Buffalo & Erie County Public Library included an art expression program as part of a 2016 Knight Foundation Grant application for their "Community Welcomes You" project. Through hands-on art classes, some run by local artists and using different mediums, participants would create works of art that express their culture and homeland, which would then be displayed at two library branches. Sadly, the library did not receive the grant, but they're trying to implement pieces of their project through other means (Buffalo & Erie County Public Library 2016).

Conversations with the Community

As you've seen, direct contact between newcomers and lifelong residents can radically change perceptions, eliminate barriers, and foster cohesion in a community. The library can offer a neutral space for these conversations to happen, either informally at any time or during a structured program. In Chapter 7, you'll examine two programs that are intended to dial directly in to difficult or challenging aspects of community conversations; this section will propose an idea for general information-sharing conversations inspired by a surprising source: the online discussion forum Reddit, best known for memes and ridiculous photos.

On Reddit, two types of posts often attract hundreds of participants and engaging discussion. One is an "Ask Me Anything" post (AMA), where a well-known public figure will offer to answer any question posted during a set time period. The other is an "I Am A" post (IAMA), where someone announces that they are a specialist or creator in a particular field—"I am a pediatrician," "I am an astrophysicist," "I am a pastry chef"—and invites questions on that particular topic for a certain amount of time. In both cases, the questions come from anyone with an account on Reddit and can frequently lead to fascinating conversations between the initiator of the post and the Reddit community.

If these models sound like they'd be well received in your area, consider finding a representative from a local organization or agency to come in and answer open questions from the community. Whether it slants more toward an AMA or an IAMA conversation depends on local interest or need. If there's a general sense of wanting to know more, bringing in someone who can speak to a particular immigrant or refugee experience and offering an AMA might be the right avenue. U.S.-born residents might want to know something general like "What's the experience of needing to leave your own country like?" or something as specific as "What's a typical breakfast in your home country?"

In contrast, an IAMA discussion might focus on the experiences of a particular type of newcomer or a person in a specific role in their cultural community. An imam might answer questions on Islam or what it's like to be a spiritual leader in a new place. A doctor might discuss what the differences are in practicing medicine in their home country versus the United States, especially in politically unstable parts of the world. A long-time U.S. lawful permanent resident in the process of applying for citizenship might discuss the experience with recent arrivals.

The topics discussed in either type of program are only limited by interest and the availability of speakers comfortable with being asked a variety of questions, some of which might be personal or trigger emotional responses. Given the unstructured nature of an AMA, in particular, it's probably a good idea to work with more seasoned speakers who can roll with any situation, or with people recommended by local organizations.

Lectures

Although they don't have the immediacy of casual, interactive events, lectures can be an objective introduction to a culture or topic related to immigrants or refugees. Academic experts, community leaders, or immigrant/refugee specialists can all provide lectures on the history of different countries and their cultural groups, holidays, language, religion, folk stories, or particular events or periods from a culture's background.

Contact local colleges to find teachers, professors, or researchers who are willing to speak on their topic of expertise, or graduate students to discuss their thesis or dissertation topics. Community and religious leaders can provide lectures as well as more discussion-oriented programs, and professionals from other countries can speak on the practice of their profession in their country of origin or anywhere their travels have taken them. Volunteers in international programs like the Peace Corps, Medicens Sans Frontiers/Doctors Without Borders, or the Red Cross/Red Crescent can describe their experiences, and those who have traveled to teach English in other countries can bring back their stories. Be aware that U.S.-born speakers will talk about life in other countries as viewed through an American lens, which is useful, but you might want to balance these accounts with the perspectives of people born in those places whenever possible.

Sister City Exchanges

Another kind of cultural sharing happens when your local community is part of a sister city exchange program. Founded by President Dwight D. Eisenhower in 1956, Sister Cities International is a nonprofit organization that oversees a membership network for sister cities in the United States, uniting tens of thousands of citizen diplomats and volunteers. "A sister city, county, or state relationship is a broad-based, long-term partnership between two communities in two countries," recognized officially by local government and composed of volunteers, nonprofits, the private sector, and civic organizations (Sister Cities n.d.).

Sister city organizations and volunteers seek to promote peace through people-to-people relationships, from pen pal/letter writing, to residency exchange programs, to shared research and development projects. Libraries can get involved in a sister city program by hosting sister city organization meetings and events, creating displays on sister cities, providing blog platforms for volunteers and staff who travel to sister cities, including letter writing as part of summer or school-year programs, and doing anything inspired by programs in this chapter.

In 2013, the Indianapolis Public Library was recognized by the Urban Libraries Council for its innovative Sister City Exchange program. Over the course of eight years, the library spotlighted each of Indianapolis' eight sister cities through library material displays, activities, and staff exchange programs. In 2013, Indianapolis partnered with the public library of Cologne, Germany, to coordinate a One Book, One City program in both cities featuring the work of Indianapolis native Kurt Vonnegut and his Cologne contemporary, Heinrich Boll. The library facilitated an online book discussion group, installed a Cologne cultural exhibit at the Central Library, and documented a library staff exchange through blog posts (http://indyplgermany.wordpress.com). Other Sister City Exchanges have included Hangzhou, China, and Campinas, Brazil (Indianapolis Public Library n.d.).

SPECIFIC TOPICS

For some cultural programs, there can be multiple approaches to highlighting topics of interest to newcomers and their receiving communities. In this section, examples based on the subject rather than the format of the program are discussed.

Personal Stories

Telling personal stories—either in writing or in person—can be one of the most compelling ways to share one's culture and allow for personal connections and understanding from one's audience. For immigrants and refugees, this is especially true, due to the disruptive experience of leaving a home and traveling hundreds or thousands of miles to relocate to a place they may have only heard of or seen via media.

Inviting newcomers to share stories of how they came to America, or of any part of their lives, is one way to cross boundaries of understanding and compassion and to put individual faces and names to stories U.S.-born citizens hear about in the news. That personal connection can be a tremendous one for storyteller and audience alike.

The type of story-sharing event a library holds depends primarily on the written literacy and comfort of the storytellers. If newcomers have sufficient written English or native language literacy, they can write their stories on their own or during a library program; these stories can then be displayed at the library, assembled into a book and circulated, or held in a local history collection. If participants don't have written literacy or would prefer and are willing to tell their stories in person, storytelling programs can be a wonderful community event. These might be in English or might be in the participants' native language, depending on their needs and who the target audience is: U.S.-born residents, other immigrants, or non-English language learners.

Thanks to a grant from the California Center for the Book, the Fresno County Public Library developed a series of programs in 2017 to allow their diverse community to share stories of coming to California. Community Librarian Michelle Gordon describes the intent of the series: "The idea is to get both the immigrant and receiving communities involved and to see our immigrants and our diversity as the positive it is. We want people to share their stories about being from somewhere other than California. It doesn't matter if home is Pittsburgh, Pennsylvania, Mexico, China, Syria or anywhere else on the globe. Most people here have come from somewhere else at some point in their family history" (Gordon 2017).

Each segment of the series invited participants to use different media to tell their stories. First, the community shared food and stories about food during a potluck of more than 20 dishes from all over the world. The next installment was virtual: the library developed an online submission form to accept (anonymous or attributed) stories of arrival and recipes for favorite dishes, which are continuously updated on the library's New Americans page (http://www.fresnolibrary.org/serv/american.html). For the third program, local 2D and 3D artists were invited to submit pieces on the theme of "coming to California" to be displayed at a library branch for a month. The finale of the series was a live storytelling event at a theater in downtown Fresno; "The California Story Jam: Until You Walk a Mile" featured 10 to 12 storytellers who shared their stories of coming to California from starting points near and far (Gordon 2017).

Another example comes from the Norwalk (CT) Public Library. It began as one woman's response to an incident in February 2017: hundreds of households in Norwalk and surrounding towns woke up to flyers containing white supremacist messages left on their driveways. Lifelong resident Sharon Baanante heard about the flyers and knew she needed to do something: "As the daughter of a predominately black father and an openly gay white mother," she says on her project's website, "I was taught at a young age to simply love everyone . . . I knew I needed to stand up for our community and for those most vulnerable during these uncertain times. The best way that I could offset the hate is by inviting my community on a journey to love ALL" (Baanante n.d.).

Two days later, Sharon launched the Love ALL Project (http://loveall project.org), a nonpartisan organization supporting diversity and fostering understanding and relationships between different cultures through inspiring sustainable collaborations. Through Love ALL, Sharon brings together local organizations to co-host an event together; by working together on and participating in the event, each organization's community would learn more about each other and, perhaps, begin to bridge even the most innocuous divides.

Vicki Oatis, Director of Youth Library Services at Norwalk Public Library, describes meeting Sharon. "I loved the project from the beginning, but she happened to come into the library about a month after she started it, and she wanted to see if we would partner with her [to develop children's programs]. We came up with the Love ALL Family Storytelling program, where we invited a local mosque to be our partner" (Oatis 2017).

(The relationship between the Norwalk Public Library and the Al Madany Islamic Center is detailed in Chapter 7.)

Attuned to their audience's needs, the Love ALL Family Storytelling evening began with a light meal shared by all participants. Families from the mosque were seated at each table, and other attendees sat down to join them; groups arriving together were encouraged to split themselves up at different tables to spread out the connections. Each table held conversation starter suggestions to break the ice, but Vicki reports they often weren't needed.

After dinner, local storyteller Karen Hall demonstrated with a few children how to develop a collaborative story, then staff distributed character and plot cards for each table to work together to write a story with a theme of love and acceptance. Says Vicki, "We had various ideas for them, like a kitten with two moms or a moose who liked to wear clothing or a monster who wasn't good at scaring people or a rainbow with no colors, things like that. They could take from the list or come up with their own idea, they had to take that and together write a story. These families came up with the most beautiful stories," and many added illustrations.

The event was a success, with approximately 80 participants and high marks in feedback; another Family Storytelling Night was planned for December 2017 (Oatis 2017).

In Boise, the focus of a similar program is on training refugees as storytellers, then giving them a platform to tell those stories. The Idaho Office for Refugees oversees the Refugee Speakers Bureau (http://www.idahorefugees .org/refugee-speakers-bureau.html), providing training for speakers from the local organization Story Story Night (www.storystorynight.org/) and coordinating speaking opportunities at public and special events through the Neighbor Narratives program. In June 2017, the Boise Public Library hosted three evenings of Neighbor Narratives at the Bown Crossing, Hillcrest, and Central libraries. Sarah Kelley-Chase, Supervisor at Bown Crossing, says, "The library supported this with space and time and advertising at all of our Boise locations for refugees to come in and tell their stories. They were really well attended and we've had requests to do more of those in the future. [A local television station] interviewed someone who had come as an audience member, who talked about how much they learned and what great insight that was" (Kelley-Chase 2017).

Media Discussion Groups

In addition to newcomers' own stories, the literary traditions of their countries of origin are compelling topics for discussion. Holding literature circles or book discussion groups in both English and other languages can equally benefit immigrants who speak those languages and learners of those other languages.

Literature Discussion Groups: English Language

Depending on staff skills, discussions around translations of work from other cultures might be easiest to implement first. These works may also already be familiar to English-speaking patrons of the library, which increases the potential for higher attendance early on in a discussion series. Rumi, a 13th-century Persian Sunni Muslim poet, scholar, mystic, and philosopher, is the focus for popular quarterly celebrations and monthly poetry discussion groups at the Boise Public Library.

Inspired by a poetry reading event, Lori Broumand, Information Services Librarian; Azam Houle, Youth Services Librarian; and Howard Olivier, private citizen (and past library board member and owner of Flying Pie Pizzeria) began the Rumi Night celebrations in 2014. These one-hour events include a Rumi poem read in English by Howard, another poem in Persian read by Azam, and an invitation to the audience to read their poems by or inspired by Rumi. Occasionally, readings are sung or accompanied by ukulele, drumming, or dancing, in keeping with diverse Persian ideas of poetic expression. After the readings, conversations continue over tea and baklava. "Everyone has a great time visiting over tea and sweet treats," says former coordinator, Joan Vestal, Information Services Librarian (now retired) at Boise's Central Library (Vestal 2017).

In February 2017, bootstrapping off the popularity of Rumi Night, a smaller group began to meet monthly to discuss and analyze Rumi's poetry. Led by Howard Olivier and Sayed Naimi, also a volunteer from Boise, the "Sohbat With Rumi" discussions are centered around stages of experience and how Rumi's poetry can be "a tool for an expression of joy as well as coping with difficulties" (Boise Public Library n.d.).

A participant at both programs submitted glowing feedback: "I'd like to thank you for the opportunity to champion two of my favorite library events: the monthly RUMI Sohbat . . . and the quarterly RUMI Night. These each in their own unique way have strengthened my sense of community . . . The broad spectrum of attendees [at the Sohbat classes] continues to surprise me. Everyone from engineers, writers, and retirees, to soothsayers, the ultra-religious, and people who read their select poems to us in Farsi . . . [Rumi Night] is even more diverse and transcends all socio-economic boundaries. It unites us via the common denominators we each are seeking: spiritual enlightenment, a greater sense of unity in this 'connected' and yet disconnected world, the deeper meaning behind the translated versions of Rumi's work, and philosophical answers to life's complex questions . . . Thank you for facilitating such a unifying experience and providing the space in which to express ourselves along with local members of our library" (Anonymous participant, via Vestal 2017).

Literature Circles: Original Language

Discussion groups about non-English literature or other popular media held in the same language as the source material give native speakers of these languages an opportunity to talk about a topic of interest and provide learners of those languages an opportunity to engage in conversation outside the classroom. In addition, by focusing on a language and not a particular country or culture, these circles can bring together people from multiple countries who share a language, from the many Spanish-speaking countries to the diverse nations in Africa and the Caribbean where French is also spoken (Haiti, Rwanda, and the Republic of Congo).

At the Louisville Free Public Library, the first Spanish Literature Circle was held nearly 10 years ago, inspired by a professor who was also a Cuban immigrant (we heard his story in Chapter 5). Lectures and discussions on literature, film, psychology, philosophy, sociology, and more are co-facilitated by librarians and patrons and are held in the original language of the material (not English). "The idea was to provide a venue for Spanish-speaking professionals and artists to share their talents with their new community," explains Sophie Maier, Immigrant Services Librarian. Eventually, the Cuban professors and writers were joined by other members of Louisville's Spanish-speaking population, who worked through cultural tensions to come together and find unity in the language. Community member Francisco Juarez, originally from Mexico, has presented on topics such as Mexican cinema and the history of native languages; some sessions feature readers' theater and interactive workshops on translation and poetry. Participants often include Spanish language students from the University of Louisville, as well as native speakers from all backgrounds.

Buoyed by the success of the Spanish Circle, a French Circle was started by a professor from West Virginia and members of Louisville's Rwandan and Congolese population; it's currently co-facilitated by Iroquois' multilingual branch manager, Valerie Viers. French Circle lectures with group discussion draw from the many different French-speaking populations in Louisville: some sessions have had more than 15 different countries represented in the room.

The Arabic Salon followed the French Circle, established by Iraqi newcomers who brought conversations on music and the healing power of poetry. Later sessions included efforts by a local Kurdish patron, Hisham Botan, to facilitate conversations on topics ranging from the social construct of race to psychology. The most recent addition to the mix is the Nepali Cultural Forum, created with the assistance of library worker Buddha Dhakal, who is a leader of the Bhutanese Society. Participants from Bhutan and Nepal engage in discussions ranging from historically well-known books to locally based authors.

For all of the discussion groups, says Sophie, "the idea is to create a safe space where people might work to preserve the relevance of their language by educating others about matters of cultural significance. No interpretation is allowed; this is for folks who are either native speakers, or fluent speakers who wish to have an immersive experience" (Maier 2017).

Book Discussion Groups

The same approach can be brought to library book discussion groups. Several libraries host Spanish language book discussion groups for both native Spanish speakers and Spanish language learners, using original Spanish language works from the many Spanish-speaking countries and translated English works of interest. Native Spanish speakers among library staff or an interested member of the community—possibly working in conjunction with a library staff person who is functional but not fluent in Spanish—can lead the programs.

You may recall the ELL Newcomers Book Club at the Rochester Hills Public Library discussed in Chapter 3. The focus of this group is as an English language conversation group, but it could easily pick up a cultural aspect for native English speakers as well by choosing English translations of well-known works from the target language. For instance, discussing works by Spanish language poets such as Pablo Neruda, Anais Nin, Frederico Garcia Lorca, or Julia de Burgos in English allows the opportunity to look at how translation by the poet and by another translator might change the subtlety of the poem's meaning. Having native speakers of both languages in the room expands the potential for learning on all sides.

Film Series

Modern film formats—DVD and Blu-ray—make it simpler and more economical than ever to host film series in many languages, for all ages. Most U.S. feature films are available with subtitles and dubbing in non-English languages; fully translated versions intended for foreign markets are available via online retailers. Many countries have strong and/or growing film industries, and those same online retailers make it more straightforward to find short pieces and feature-length films in those native languages.

Festivals of Short Films

For decades, the National Film Board of Canada has supported the creation of high-quality films relevant to Canadian life and culture. Unfortunately for libraries, these films were often prohibitively expensive to buy on VHS or even DVD. Today, online video sources such as Vimeo (www.vimeo.com) or the film board's own website (http://www.nfb.ca/) can be a source for videos to show and discuss in a library program. These series could focus on a particular language, country, theme, or style of filmmaking—whatever might be of most interest to your users.

Most countries have an equivalent of the National Film Board of Canada; search for "national film board" and the country you're interested in to find the appropriate government agency for that location.

Local filmmakers, including those from newcomer communities, are nearly always looking for venues to show their work. Seek out student films, independent filmmakers, and locally produced documentaries for film series content. At the time she was interviewed, Sophie Maier had a documentary on the history of Arab Americans in the United States on her desk, which she was featuring later in the year; the library has also shown a documentary about refugees in Louisville—*My New Kentucky Home*— produced by an English Conversation Club volunteer who is also a film-maker (Maier 2017).

One thing that is more relevant for a film series than nonvisual media is the occasionally very different attitudes cultures have toward nudity, language, sex, and violence depicted in films. What may be perfectly acceptable in an American romance "chick flick" might be problematic for viewers from India, and what is fine in animation targeted at Japanese children might make American parents uncomfortable. None of these are reasons to *not* show these films, but awareness of these cultural differences will help library staff deal with any questions or concerns that come up.

Music Sharing and Discussion

An outgrowth of Louisville's Cultural Showcases is the Music Show-cases, specific opportunities for musicians of all traditions to perform and talk about the music of their lives. Sophie coordinated the first Music Showcase, but when it was populated almost entirely by teenagers, she handed over the reins for the second. "I just let them work on the logistics and emcee and take control over it," she says, "and that was really great" (Maier 2017).

Music-centered programs can follow any model, from small group discussion to large performances, and include storytelling or dance as well as food and informal conversation. Music lends itself to any situation, so include it in other events as you can.

Non-English Conversation Groups

When discussing English language learning, we looked at English language conversation groups as a way for learners to practice in less formal, more interest-directed environments. Conversation groups in languages other than English provide the same for both native speakers of those languages and English speakers who are trying to learn. These conversation groups might be two-way or might stay focused tightly on the non-English language, depending on interest and skill of the participants.

Conversation groups might be simply a meeting space to "practice conversational Spanish," or they might be intended to foster discussions between community members who share that language but come from different countries of origin (as with the literature circles discussed earlier). They could be a learning opportunity or an informal chat session, with pre-chosen topics or self-generated tangents, led by a trained facilitator or group-led. Anything goes, really, and the same group can evolve over time as the participants, their interests, or their needs do. Allowing for flexibility and open-endedness in such a program can keep it relevant as time passes and the demographics of the local immigrant or refugee populations shift.

Cooking Programs

Never underestimate the power of food to bring people together. As with the media discussion or conversation practice groups, programs organized around sharing food and cooking styles are perfect opportunities for informal discussion on a shared context. Cultural notes and different words for the same ingredients or cooking methods will weave in and around cookbook discussions and cooking demonstrations, as will personal stories.

At the Iroquois Branch, Sophie has invited local restaurateurs from different countries to co-present with a chef who also teaches; the chef discusses the cultural aspects of the cuisine from an academic perspective, and the restaurateur describes their experiences in cooking.

As part of Fresno County Public Library's "Coming to California" series, they held a potluck with food contributed by community members. Each dish was accompanied by a list of ingredients, information about where the dish came from, and any stories participants wanted to share about the food or their experiences. More than 20 unique dishes fed 45 people while a curated Freegal playlist of music from around the world served as a background. The meal was incredibly eclectic (cultures included where known): zwieback and cardamom breads, chili, mashed potatoes, finger sandwiches, southern greens and turnips, macaroni salad, two different rice side dishes, danh-hoon (Vietnamese/Cambodian noodles), isso wade and parippu wade (Sri Lankan shrimp patties and lentil patties, respectively), baked chicken, a sopes station (a Mexican dish involving a thick fried masa base covered with different toppings), a Hawaiian pork sandwich station—and those were just the savory dishes! Desserts included Swedish butter cookies, apple pie, tres leches cake, and peanut butter pie.

Feedback from the event included many thanks to the library for providing a "calm and friendly" atmosphere to share stories and described how "nice and interesting [it was] to see and taste foods from different cultures." Participants at the event and afterwards asked when the next potluck would be held (Gordon 2017).

Again, if your library has limitations around preparing or serving food in the building, work within those constraints or use this as an opportunity to re-examine them.

Discussions about Spirituality

At the beginning of this chapter, there was a brief mention of the fact that many cultures outside the United States intertwine religion and daily life more closely than Americans often do. Another way to share those cultures is to actively explore them through their religion: its philosophies, values, practices, and guidelines for interacting with others.

Boise's Rumi discussion comes close to this kind of program, but Sarah Kelley-Chase is hoping to try a more direct approach at the new Bown Crossing branch. The city of Boise has introduced new evaluation criteria for city buildings, a health impact survey that looks at seven dimensions in the areas around any proposed new buildings (you'll look at this again in the next chapter). Says Sarah, "One of the dimensions is Spiritual, which is an interesting challenge for libraries to be a platform to present conversations and start conversations."

Her idea for Bown involves a series of discussion groups that examines different faiths, including some that aren't as well known, to provide opportunities for clarity and conversation. Potentially held on a monthly basis, different presenters would facilitate each group and encourage participants to journal about their thoughts and perspectives during the series. Sarah admits, "It's kind of lofty, and it would take a lot of dedication on the part of those participating, but I think it would be a really interesting way for the library to continue to serve as a safe space to have a conversation and to ask questions and to share and to learn" (Kelley-Chase 2017).

In Chapter 7, you'll explore other ways for libraries to be that safe space and help build the community around them.

SUMMING UP

One of the great strengths of libraries has always been as places to explore the world without leaving your town, and by including programs that celebrate the rich diversity of cultures now found in many communities, libraries can be even more accessible "windows to the world." There are dozens of focuses for cultural celebrations and learning opportunities in libraries, each customizable to suit the needs and interests of the local receiving and newcomer communities:

- Exhibitions and displays of library materials or local artists' work
- Cultural showcases and lectures highlighting local immigrant populations
- Craft, music, food, or dance programs
- Discussion groups for any type of media
- Participation in Sister City exchanges
- Community conversations about culture, personal stories, and religion

The final two chapters will build on the inspirations discussed to this point and show you how to use outreach and partnerships to build community and find the support needed to develop and expand services to immigrants and new Americans.

7

$\diamond$ $\diamond$ $\diamond$

BUILDING COMMUNITY

Chapters 2 through 6 introduced the three pillars of immigration integration (language, civic, economic) and explored how library programs and services can address these needs and discussed ways for the library to celebrate the diverse cultures of newcomers and lifelong residents alike. These last two chapters will shift gears to illustrate steps libraries can take to become a central point of community building around newcomers and expand services.

You've now seen many examples of libraries being integral to building bridges between newcomers and their receiving communities through programs centered around other topics. In this chapter, you'll zero in on activities explicitly designed to strengthen those bridges.

BUILDING COMMUNITY THROUGH OUTREACH

Of the many ways library staff have been asked to adapt to the changing nature of the field, one change is often particularly difficult: you need to get out of your building and meet people where they are. This has always been true, to some extent, and is even more so in the mobile and scattered reality of 21st-century American life. Expecting those who are new to the country—who may have different ideas or no idea of what a public library is and what they offer—to simply walk in our doors because we're here is even more unrealistic than for U.S.-born residents. You have to go to them, especially in the beginning of the relationship.

Just such a beginning happened when two Norwalk (CT) Public Library staff walked up the street to the new Al Madany Islamic Center's first open house. Vicki Oatis, Norwalk's director of youth services; Moina Noor, a member of the mosque who also sits on the library board; and Sharon Baanante, founder of the Love ALL project, tell their versions of this beginning.

Vicki: "I knew [the mosque had] had a hard time getting a space here in Norwalk, but they finally did and it turns out it was right down the street from our library, in an old church. The mosque was hosting their first open house and I wanted to go because I had never been to a mosque. I thought it would be fascinating to go and meet the people and get an insight to their culture that way . . . What made [my co-worker Evelyn and I] so happy initially is that it was very crowded; there were a lot of people attending and that made us proud of our community . . . We walked in and I don't think we ever realized how many people we knew from the library who belonged to the mosque! . . . We got lots of hugs when we walked in and people seemed just very excited to have us there, which made us feel good and made us even happier that we went." Vicki and Evelyn observed prayers ("It was so beautiful . . . and the children do what they have to do [while the adults pray]"), toured the mosque, and enjoyed activities like wrapping headscarves and getting temporary henna tattoos. Vicki's family joined them and "we ended up staying an hour past when they were done because my kids were having such a good time."

During and after the visit, Vicki noted how members of the mosque responded to the visit by the librarians. "A wonderful woman—Hannan, who brings her two children to the library all the time and who we've always had a nice relationship with—immediately became all teary-eyed when she saw us, which made us feel good for going . . . She said she had meant to come to the library and personally invite us, but things got so busy that she didn't, so she couldn't believe we just showed up on our own. It meant a lot to her, clearly, that we were there; she wrote us thank you cards later." Another woman who had been pleasant during her visits to the library warmed up after the open house. "Now she wants to stand and chat with us and she smiles at us. I think she always thought that we were nice because that was our job, but I think there's just this feeling of trust now. She feels that, ok, we wanted to get to know her and her culture and religion better, and I think now she feels like she can be more open with us. I don't know if it was that she couldn't trust us completely, but now there's definitely this warmer relationship that makes us feel good" (Oatis 2017).

Moina: "I grew up in Norwalk. I left for a while and came back [but] my family has been long-term library users, now . . . I sit on the library board of trustees. In February 2016, we—the Muslim community of Norwalk—acquired a property down the street from the library. Our community is made up of some people who grew up in the United States, but a good 70–75% of our congregation are immigrants from all corners of the world, especially South Asia, Africa, and the Middle East. We have a congregation of roughly 100 families, and it's been growing since we acquired the property. One of our missions, aside from providing a space for spiritual and daily practice, [was to be accessible]. . . . We wanted to use this space as a home base for outreach work, for people to learn more about Islam [and] Muslims and being part of the civic life of the city.

(continued)

One relationship we wanted to build was the one with the local library because they have been so open to members of the Muslim community. Every single time I go there, I'll see someone there from the mosque there with their kids. People like Vicki and other librarians, they're so warm and hospitable; a lot of people have been taking English classes there, and now, we're a neighbor.

"[The mosque] had an open house in March of 2017, and we made a very special point to invite all of the library staff and members of the board of the library. We put a lot of effort into this open house. We had a whole section on books: one woman in our congregation is a collector of youth literature . . . [The open house] almost felt like a library program in that way because it had [an] educational, artistic, cultural component to it.

Through that event, there were a lot of nice partnerships made. One was with an organization called the Love All project; they've also been very supportive. [Also,] the church down the street recently joined with another church and they're [restructuring their congregation]; we met them and lots of other neighbors . . . Once people know that you're open to these things, partnerships and alliances build.

When Vicki and Sharon had the idea to do a family storytelling night, they asked us to be a co-sponsor. That was such a nice collaborative project. All it really entails was for us to get people there, and we did! There were so many of [our community] that came; that type of programming is so great and I'm hopeful that we can do more of it.

I feel like [Norwalk Director] Christine Bradley and Vicki are connectors, in a way. They bring different groups of people together, and because we're a neighbor and we're there, we're really looking forward to more connections with other different groups [facilitated in part by the library]" (Noor 2017).

Sharon: "Collaborating with the Norwalk Public Library was exemplary. The [library's] community values and physical space were essential to achieving Love ALL Project's mission of fostering relationships between different cultures. The public library has an organic ability to connect with an expansive range of Norwalk residents from different cultures, socioeconomic backgrounds, and ages. They also have the ability to host events in a very unbiased way, meaning with no political affiliation or agenda. To many, including Love ALL Project and cultural organizations, the library is a safe neutral environment that is welcoming to everyone.

I would love to continue working with the library to see how we can help them embed diversity into their programming. I would encourage the Norwalk Public Library (and libraries around the country) to consider changing some of the topics of existing programs to diversity focused topics. Most importantly, I would recommend that they use Love ALL Project's framework and partner with two cultural organizations for each diversity program. Diversity programming and connecting with community organizations will contribute directly to the library's sustainability. In addition to the sustainability benefits of this framework, the library will gain a larger audience, will build trust with community organizations and will organically create a platform for intercultural relationships and support" (Baanante 2017).

Sophie Maier of Louisville is especially dedicated to the task of going to where her audiences are: "Other outreach involves finding newcomers, making them library cards, getting them into the library and finding out how we can best all work together. That's going into the refugee resettlement agencies, adult English classes, workplace things, religious [and] cultural events out in the community. Tabling all the time. Just, basically, whenever there's any community event that somehow involves immigrants or, sometimes, [events centered on] racial justice because I want to get my foot in the door there, too, and make it all relevant." At a local mosque's open house, for example, "We were set up inside the mosque, bringing books to learn Arabic because that population has more Indian and Pakistani Muslims, so they want to learn Arabic and teach their children Arabic, as well as cookbooks on Syrian foods. Of course, books for adults in Arabic, which completely freak people out, they are so surprised we have those" (Maier 2017).

The Grand Tour

Of course, as soon as you go out, you can invite them right back in again. The San Diego Public Library has developed a partnership with the Southwest Key Immigrant Youth Shelter, a service focused on providing unaccompanied migrant youth housing and referrals to other services. (For more on Southwest Key's programs across the country, visit http://www.swkey.org.)

"We first met with instructors at the shelter to find out how the library could support their unique curriculum," says Adriana (Ady) Huertas, Manager at San Diego's Logan Heights branch. Youth might be at the shelter for as little as a week or up to three months, giving library staff little time to make connections with them individually. After an initial meeting with shelter staff, the library began inviting groups of youth from the shelter to the Central Library and Logan Heights Branch for library tours in Spanish, unusual projects such as an identity drawing exercise, and an off-site Summer Reading program. Ady explains, "[T]he goal of the visits was to introduce and connect refugee and immigrant youth to the library . . . and for them to know that wherever they end up in the country, their local library is a friendly, welcoming, safe institution where they can find resources that can help them with their education, information, and personal needs and interests" (Koerber 2016 A).

At each visit, teen library staff hand out relevant materials and promotional flyers, give teens a two-hour tour of the library with an emphasis on the teen space, and encourage the teens to see the library as a safe place to come and be themselves. The message is reinforced through free books provided to residents of the shelter that contain an insert with information about resources available to them in the library; the books come from donations to the REFORMA Children in Crisis Task Force project (Huertas 2016).

Mobile Promotion

As part of the national push to get out where nonusers can see you, libraries have developed innovative ways of taking it to the streets . . . and to town fairs, farmers markets, and outdoor festivals. You can use these tools at any outdoor gathering or remote location, but a few that will maximize your exposure to immigrants and other newcomers include:

- Cultural festivals and parades
- Town/county fairs
- School open houses
- Large naturalization ceremonies (again, check with your local United States Citizenship and Immigration Services [USCIS] field office first)
- Farmers markets or produce markets
- Craft fairs, especially if they have a specific cultural theme
- Community center events
- Shopping district celebrations in immigrant-heavy neighborhoods

Biblio Bicycles

In urban centers, the image of a bicycle messenger zooming by or a pedicab driver ringing a bell through an intersection is a fairly common sight. Bicycles make sense in a city, requiring no fuel (other than food for the rider) and little space to park. If your service area is urban, small, or vehicle free, a biblio bicycle is a relatively low-cost investment that dramatically increases your outreach range.

In 2014, the Boston Public Library first introduced the Bibliocycle, a human-powered outreach vehicle that's perfect for crowded city events. A small crew of dedicated cyclist staff volunteer for Bibliocycle shifts, pedaling a cartload of library items, promotional materials, computers to demonstrate online resources, and library card sign-up tools to farmers' markets, neighborhood celebrations, and anywhere else they can go (Boston Public Library 2014).

Electric, Agile, Fun!

When the Grandview Heights Public Library (GHPL) in Ohio was considering how to increase their range for outreach activities—a biblio bicycle was too limited, a bookmobile too large—GHPL Director Ryan McDonnell was inspired by the food truck boom and did a little research.

"A low-speed vehicle is ideal for our small service area," he explains. "It has an exceptional 'green' rating, is a fraction of the cost of a standard bookmobile, and is an exciting way to engage the community" (Koerber 2016 B).

McDonnell and library staff worked with library volunteer Mike Dexter (who donated his time and expertise) on the graphic design and local vehicle customization firm All-A-Cart on the construction to bring the mobile library to life; total cost for the vehicle, customization, and supplies was around $50,000, paid for by the Grandview Heights Public Library Foundation. Roughly the size of a small delivery van, the PopUp mobile library can be driven by anyone with a standard driver's license; a pool of 20 trained staff use an online schedule to sign up for shifts. The electric engine can be charged using a standard 110-volt outlet, and the truck is licensed for use on public roads but lightweight, so it can be driven to an event and parked on a street, field, park, or sidewalk as needed.

The rear of the truck has large display shelving to show off books even while it's moving—perfect for parades!—and storage compartments for plastic tables and chairs, a step ladder, marketing materials, and other equipment. Staff bring a library laptop and smartphone (for a wireless hotspot connection if needed) to access the ILS, so visitors can sign up for library cards, check out materials from the truck, place items on hold, and update their account information (Koerber 2016 B).

"Staff love getting out in the community and working special events," says Canaan Faulkner, GHPL Public Relations Manager. "The response from the community has been overwhelmingly positive. It's been amazing to connect with new people and incoming residents . . . not only is it a great service tool, but a great marketing tool as well" (Faulkner 2016). GHPL Youth Services Manager Eileen McNeil enjoys the interaction with the public: "When we take the PopUp Library to the parks, it's hard not to smile. Usually there are kids sitting around on the curbs or in the grass, completely immersed in the book they just found. This creates a contagious desire to grab a book, sit under a tree, and get lost in the pages" (Koerber 2016 B).

For more on the PopUp Library, visit the library's web page (http://www .ghpl.org/2015/06/01/ghpl-popup-library/) or read the article on it in *Library Journal* (http://lj.libraryjournal.com/2016/11/opinion/one-cool-thing/its -electric-one-cool-thing/).

Mobile Services, 21st-Century Edition

Through the affordances of 21st-century technologies, the library bookmobile is undergoing a renaissance and can be a vital tool in reaching newcomer communities. Again, this is resource multitasking at its finest, because the same vehicles can be used for serving residence-bound, homeless, and school-based customers.

Traditional bookmobiles are still alive and well and can be brought to housing developments, community centers, and organizations that work with immigrant and refugee families. They might be less intimidating than a library building, especially overwhelmingly complex, large, urban central libraries. New residents can get library cards, hear more about services, and browse the bookmobile collections, gradually acclimating to the idea of a public library and what it offers if they aren't already familiar.

Newer outreach vehicles go beyond materials to bring more of the library's services outside its buildings. The Houston Public Library's (HPL) Mobile Express is a "computer classroom on wheels" and brings technology and related programs to high-need neighborhoods. Using the lab's computers, Wi-Fi, and large-screen digital whiteboard, the Community Engagement Team offers literacy programs, workforce development training, computer training, homework help, enrichment programs, ESL classes, afterschool programs, and library card registration anywhere the bus can travel. They work directly with community partner organizations who request visits from HPL Mobile Express, including high schools, community centers, apartment complexes, other city departments, churches, and nonprofit organizations.

MyTesha Tates, Community Engagement Manager, ascribes the success of the program to its flexibility: "The most important aspect of [what we do] has been our ability to go into areas of the community, many of whom would not have access to library services or technology otherwise. Without the flexibility that our mobility affords us, so many people wouldn't be able to take advantage of the classes we offer. Our classes equip our customers with the skills that they need" to enter the workforce and engage with all aspects of life in the United States (Tates 2016).

The Learn and Play bus program developed by the Topeka & Shawnee County Public Library is a mobile outreach vehicle designed for children ages birth to six years and their caregivers. Created as a result of community focus groups, the Learn and Play bus is designed to reduce the disparity in early learning experiences for children entering kindergarten. Marie Pyko, Director of Public Services, explains its origin: "Fifty-five percent of children in Topeka & Shawnee County enter kindergarten with no preschool experience and often not only know fewer words than their classmates but also struggle with sharing and taking turns. [During the focus group process], one principal expressed, 'Can you imagine where we could go if all children had an early learning experience and started in a similar place for kindergarten?'" (Pyko 2017).

The library worked with a group of early learning educators to develop a curriculum based on the ones used at local preschools and, through library foundation and private funding, bought and fitted out a 40-foot diesel bus with a multipurpose activity space. The Learn & Play Bus makes weekly 1- to 2.5-hour visits to neighborhoods throughout Topeka and Shawnee County. Pyko explains, "Families who visit the bus have an opportunity to listen and interact during story time, play with early learning toys, and engage in messy art activities." Handouts reinforce the learning and suggest fun family activities to do at home.

Community learning experts are on hand to educate caregivers on language development, nutrition, or other health questions through casual conversations rather than lectures. "The goal is to be an informal and comfortable space so that caregivers have opportunities to just talk with experts and be their child's best teacher," adds Pyko. In its first six months, the Learn & Play Bus reached over 250 families, and staff saw marked improvement in frequent visitors' attention, language development, and social-emotional skills (Pyko 2017).

BUILDING COMMUNITY THROUGH PARTNERSHIPS

As you'll see again in Chapter 8, leveraging the power of partnerships is a crucial part of providing services to immigrants and refugees. Personal recommendations and referrals from agencies those communities trust carry more weight than any number of media releases or flyer campaigns. In addition, developing partnerships with organizations that serve newcomers is often a two-way exchange: organizations promote library services to their clients and can provide services and presenters for library programs, and libraries can refer users to the organizations and be a location for extended services.

The best part of partnerships is that, with some effort at maintenance, the network only gets larger over time. According to Assistant Deputy Director Dawn Peters, the Buffalo & Erie County Public Library system has more than 700 partner organizations; imagine the reach a single email sent to that list could have, if even half pass it on to the people they serve! "The library has established and continues to build relationships with agencies that directly work with immigrants, refugees, and new Americans, including the International Institute of Buffalo; Jericho Road; Journey's End; Erie County New Americans Committee; City of Buffalo Office of New Americans; Literacy New York; and many more," says Peters. She also expands on the benefits of those efforts: "Building relationships with the local schools, agencies, and the city and county, and supporting each other's initiatives, has helped with referrals and getting the word out [including to] undocumented persons. Working together has also educated staff on the concerns, fears, and apprehensions of the immigrants/refugees/new Americans. This education helps staff to understand the needs of these populations and plan and prepare programs accordingly" (Peters 2017).

Making Connections

It all starts with getting out and into other spaces than the ones you may be used to. Part of the library director's role has typically been to serve as an institutional outreach liaison to boards, committees, commissions, philanthropies, and nonprofit organizations with the aim of increasing awareness of the library's offerings and needs. That responsibility can— and should—be shared with other staff in an effort to be in more places. Branch managers, outreach staff, dedicated immigrant or workforce development staff, and youth librarians are all prime candidates to be an ear and voice for the library, serving as board and committee members and liaisons. Another avenue is to attend city- or county-wide events and trainings and pay attention to networking opportunities, because sometimes, simply being in the room with the right person at the right time can be enough.

Maddy Ildefonso from Los Angeles Public Library was attending a citywide "Know Your Rights" training and the discussion turned to State Bill 54 (SB-54), the California Values Act. The text of the act was on the screen, and Maddy noticed that libraries weren't included in the list of "safe zones": public spaces that the state government intends to ensure "remain safe and accessible to all California residents, regardless of immigrant status." The oversight bothered Maddy enough to push her to speak up: "It's just funny that libraries are frequently left out of the conversation, so I raised my hand and asked the room, 'You know, it'd be great if somebody could remember to include libraries, and how do we go about doing that, to be better advocates when something like this comes up?'"

As it happened, a policy director from the national group Asian Americans Advancing Justice was also attending the training; she volunteered to ask her team working in the senator's office if they could get libraries on the list, and it worked. Maddy was thrilled she had spoken up. "I didn't know there was a policy director in the room . . . It takes those people to be plugged in, too, because once I asked that question, the policy director [exclaimed], 'Oh my goodness! How on earth did we not get libraries?

How did we miss that? I love libraries! Libraries are everything—how did we miss that?'" (Ildefonso 2017).

The current text of SB-54 now reads: "The Attorney General, by October 1, 2018, in consultation with the appropriate stakeholders, shall publish model policies limiting assistance with immigration enforcement to the fullest extent possible consistent with federal and state law at public schools, *public libraries*, health facilities operated by the state or a political subdivision of the state, courthouses, Division of Labor Standards Enforcement facilities, the Agricultural Labor Relations Board, the Division of Workers Compensation, and shelters, and ensuring that they remain safe and accessible to all California residents, regardless of immigration status" (SB-54 2016).

For Alicia Moguel, building partnerships is the "bread and butter" of her work in the Department of Lifelong Learning at Los Angeles Public Library. "We're very involved in working with all the local nonprofits. We're part of the California Community Foundation Task Force, which includes a lot of community-based organizations that work with immigrant integration programs [and] services. We also work closely with our Mayor's Office of Immigrant Affairs, attending meetings and connecting with nonprofits. That's how we developed our program early on and continue to build on it, by making these connections, which will now be extremely helpful in the work that we do moving forward with our DOJ recognition and accreditation" (Moguel 2017).

When attending these meetings and trainings, always be genuine and honest about what the library can and can't offer. It's a truth that libraries have limited resources and that as a public service, they must remain politically neutral. Local and state governments may have ethics guidelines in place that specify what municipal employees can and cannot do with regard to social, political, or religious affairs. As a participant of these boards and committees, set and maintain the boundaries you need to both be active in the space and work within the rules you're subject to. If "all" you can do is suggest what the group can do to help the library or listen and bring back information to the library that can shape priorities and program development, the effort is worth it.

Sophie Maier of Louisville considers this as much a core part of her work as running the English Conversation Clubs. She spends a fair amount of time "serving on different boards and committees around town, and trying to do trainings for other metro government agencies, such as social service workers who work with immigrants and refugees. I also go into U.S.-born dominated religious institutions with the same spiel and, while I have no way to 'force' them to volunteer [like the college students], I can just say that it would be an altruistic thing for you good religious people to come and volunteer" (Maier 2017).

Attending these meetings can provide networking opportunities to get potential partners excited and engaged in what the library is doing. Ask them what they and their constituents need, and seek input on possible programs and services. Once you've established that you're willing to make that effort to come and participate in their meetings and trainings, invite them to sit in on focus groups, planning discussions, trainings, or tours at the library to find out what you have or are thinking of offering. These conversations are a chance to understand the needs of different populations from the questions they ask as they explore the library and its services.

Potential Partners

To say that there are dozens of potential partners for serving newcomer populations—even in small towns—is a vast understatement. Local government, nonprofits, and other organizations may be working with these communities, as well as state and national initiatives working on local projects. With this many possibilities, where do you start, and who do you focus on?

Other Libraries

An obvious choice is partnering with nearby libraries, either other publics or reaching out to school, college, or special libraries in the area. Even if these libraries are not part of a formal network or consortium with your library, you can benefit from exchanging ideas and sharing resources to serve the same or similar newcomer populations.

The Hartford Public Library is part of a partnership of seven libraries across the state of Connecticut. Homa Naficy, Executive Director of The American Place at Hartford Public Library, describes the project: "As part of a USCIS grant, a [library peer partnership of seven libraries is] working together to increase and improve a uniform message and share/exchange ideas. On Library Week in April of 2018, we want to host naturalization ceremonies at all of these libraries at the same time, to increase visibility as an institution, and as a welcoming resource center for immigrants." Based on the success of The American Place, Hartford is spearheading the effort to help their partners build their citizenship collections and programs, and is working a little more closely with the Norwich and Stamford libraries to offer classes there. "We're meeting with our colleagues on a regular basis, trying to build their capacity as far as funding, [including] grants they can get through USCIS or the Department of Education" (Naficy 2017).

City and Regional Administrators

Within local government, many different departments touch on services to immigrants, refugees, and new Americans. Neighborhood development, social services, police, small business, and workforce development— we've seen multiple examples of libraries working across municipal departments to provide resources and programs to newcomers.

David Leonard, President of the Boston Public Library, outlines this relationship: "Boston Public Library as a city department is an integral part of city administration and may provide recommendations during policy discussions. City policy is set by the Mayor's Office with consideration given to how all City departments can be supportive when new policy is implemented. The library is in constant contact with city colleagues on how to ensure our shared resources continue to be available to all members of our community, and that the Boston Public Library will remain a place where all may feel welcome. The library has a longstanding relationship with the City's Office of Immigrant Advancement, which works to strength the ability of immigrants and Boston's diverse cultural and linguistic communities to fully participate in the economic, civic, social, and cultural life of Boston. Our collaboration with the agency has continued to deepen in this time period, specifically around communicating to our immigrant and refugee communities about the materials and services available to them at their local library branches" (Leonard 2017).

In Somerville, Director Glenn Ferdman described an ongoing series of conversations on diversity and equality led by the city's Inclusion and Diversity Coordinator/ADA Compliance Coordinator; participants have included city staff from various departments, including the library. He adds, "Black Lives Matter has been involved, as has the Cambridge Health Alliance. This was an outgrowth [of] the city's conversations on race and racism back in the summer of 2015, preceding the current federal administration" (Ferdman 2017). The Inclusion and Diversity Department also contains SomerViva, a trio of Spanish-, Portuguese-, and Haitian Kreyol–speaking liaisons working to "connect immigrant residents with City services, engage them in public processes, and celebrate the city's diverse cultures" (SomerViva n.d.).

Occasionally, the library can help create a government partner where it didn't exist before. In Hartford, an immigrant advisory group that met at the library wanted to shift focus from information to advocacy. Although the library recognized that they could not advocate directly on behalf of immigrants, they could—and did—support the advisory group as they formalized into a commission. Homa clarifies this choice: "This is [a way] that the library can help—we serve as a catalyst. We serve everyone. You identify needs, and you try and create a path or ways for people to obtain the information they need to achieve what it is. Instead of going out and advocating, we created a path so that advocacy for immigrants could happen."

The library continued to provide a meeting space for the group, helped them find information on becoming a city commission, and invited a representative from the city to talk with the group about the process. Now, the Commission on Immigrant and Refugee Affairs runs independently, though they do still meet at the library and the library continues to offer some technology support (Naficy 2017).

Organizations Serving Newcomers

Clearly, organizations already serving immigrants and refugees are exceptional partners for library efforts to do the same. These organizations can be incredibly responsive to offers of and requests for help, and shared missions to service make aligning goals straightforward.

MyTesha Tates, Community Outreach Manager for Houston's mobile service, explains the library's view: "We've also reached out to organizations that share our goals and partner with them to reach members of the community. It helps us because these organizations have already made connections, they have audiences in place already. We just have to create that relationship between the library and the organization, so that we can serve our customers where they eat, sleep, and play. It's a win-win scenario that benefits the library, our partner organizations, and the people we serve" (Tates 2016).

In Topeka, developing the Learn and Play bus taught them a similar lesson. "A shared goal and shared project builds a strong coalition of supporters and actual doers for the success of a project," says Library Director Marie Pyko. "Everyone brings their expertise to the table, and when community partners are there from the very beginning, the sky is the limit on what they will do to help make the service successful." Enthuses Pyko, "Our community partners not only helped us envision . . . the new service, they all agreed to be . . . shared collaborators of this project and the community impact goal" (Pyko 2017).

Los Angeles Public Library is currently at a very different point in their process: the Department of Lifelong Learning is trying to identify and build on existing relationships with other organizations. Alicia Moguel, Associate Director of the department, explains, "What we're trying to do is look at all of the initiatives that fall under our department: city-wide, system-wide initiatives of the library, including those on health and financial literacy." The library initiated partnerships with groups like the Children's Bureau and the county Department of Public Social Services to develop the Health Matters initiative, which helps people access health insurance, organizes health screenings and flu clinics, supports workshops on health literacy topics, and provides case management and health screenings for the homeless.

Alicia turned to these partners again when an initiative came out of the mayor's office related to the adoption of a California Senate Bill, Health for All Kids, which provides coverage for persons under the age of 19, regardless of immigration status. Says Alicia, "Their target group was the kids of immigrants, mixed-status families, with children who don't have health care . . . We worked with Department of Public Social Services in all of our libraries to reach that population, so [the effort overlapped with] our citizenship/new Americans initiative and our Health Matters initiative. We were reaching mixed-status families so that they know they're a part of our community and could take advantage of this. A lot of our programs and services can intersect, because we try to serve the whole family." The library also made use of its partnerships with health centers that serve anyone, regardless of immigration status (Moguel 2017).

During the creation of the Paschalville Partnership in Philadelphia, community partners showed an understanding that libraries and non-profit organizations frequently have compatible missions that benefit from strong partnerships. Philadelphia Works is a workforce development organization that is one of the Paschalville partners; Chief Research Officer Meg Shope Koppel says, "Libraries are great community outreach sites for workforce services and can help get career seekers started . . . Many workforce development boards are building web-based platforms, [and libraries] can provide technical support and learning opportunities on how to best use these." Grant providers are also more likely to approve grants for projects that already show significant local support, Philadelphia Works discovered. "[We] wrote a grant and received funding . . . leveraging [the library's] existing bootcamps. Cooperative grant opportunities that align with the mission of the project can really enhance efforts and provide momentum," adds Meg (Koerber 2016 C).

The Networks for Integrating New Americans project described in Chapter 1 provides multiple examples of these partnerships in action. In Rhode Island, Karisa Tashjian, Director of Education at Providence Public Library and Director of RIFLI, notes that the ALLAccess Learning Lounges are also "an ideal space for inviting community partners to provide their services to new audiences . . . This has led to a fantastic partnership with the House of Hope and RI Coalition for the Homeless" (Tashjian 2016).

Through the NINA project, the Fresno County Public Library developed partnerships with the Fresno Adult School and the Central Valley Immigrant Integration Collaborative (CVICC). Says Community Librarian Michelle Gordon, "The library will often have an information table at a lot of their DACA and Naturalization workshops and their Medical enrollments fairs" (Gordon 2017).

Finally, the Neighbors United Subcommittee on Adult Education continues to be a great opportunity for Boise Public Library to network and collaborate with other refugee-serving organizations, including both educational institutions and resettlement agencies. "This year, we have focused our committee work on developing new objectives and goals to ensure we are serving our three primary audiences: refugees, educators, and our community," says Renee Addington, Branch Librarian at Boise's Library! at Bown Crossing. "We have a program coming up in September to provide more information and support to refugees interested [in] the College of Western Idaho, and we hope to offer a similar program this fall for Boise State University" (Addington 2017).

Welcoming America

Building local partnerships from the ground up has the benefit of local focus and intentionality, but there are also existing national networks and initiatives to tap into. One of the largest and most centered around immigrants and refugees is Welcoming America, a nonprofit, nonpartisan organization dedicated to spreading the Welcoming Community movement on a global scale. "A Welcoming Community is one that has made a commitment to develop a community culture and political environment that encourages newcomers of all backgrounds to feel valued and fully integrate into the social, civic, and economic fabric of their new homes" (Welcoming America n.d. A); the goal is growing the vibrancy and prosperity of the city or town through these contributions. Seeking a broader base than a single program or service can provide, Welcoming America staff work with multiple institutions in a community to build bridges and reduce the barriers newcomers face to that integration.

Launched in 2009, Welcoming America provides networks, training, resources, leveraged funding, and coordinated events such as Welcoming Week to create and support connections between participating organizations. Members of the Welcoming America network can be any local government or nonprofit "who is willing to commit to planning, building, and sustaining the ongoing inclusion and long-term economic and social integration of newcomers, as well as communicating messages of unity and shared values to the community" (Welcoming America n.d. A).

Welcoming America offers a variety of ways that a community can be involved in and benefit from this initiative (Welcoming America n.d. A):

- **Welcoming Cities and Counties Network:** By becoming Welcoming America participants, cities, counties, and nonprofit organizations have access to online resources, informational lists, and learning exchanges with other participants locally, nationally, and globally. View a map of current members at http://www.welcomingamerica.org/programs/our-network.

- **Welcoming Institute:** Through online and in-person trainings, workshops, proactive and reactive technical assistance, and resources, Welcoming America offers education in leadership and communication, economic opportunity and education, civic engagement, equitable access, and safe and connected communities—the five elements of the Welcoming America framework.

- **Certified Welcoming and the Welcoming Standard:** To help cities and communities improve their ability to provide a welcoming environment for all, Welcoming America offers local governments the opportunity to self-assess and undergo an evaluation that will identify strengths and show areas for growth. The evaluation is based on the Welcoming Standard, guidelines built by Welcoming America and its participating organizations to be a framework for immigrant inclusion.

- **Welcoming Refugees:** An initiative that focuses the general principles of Welcoming America specifically on how receiving communities can be more inclusive of new refugees.

- **Welcoming Week:** During a week in September, Welcoming America promotes and supports events around the country that "bring together immigrants, refugees, and native-born residents to raise awareness of the benefits of welcoming everyone" (Welcoming America n.d. B). Events include festivals, volunteer projects, shared dinners, or any event that encourages connectivity and dialogue. (The next section will look more closely at this type of program, but the Norwalk Family Storytelling Night is another fantastic example.)

- **Resources to Support Welcoming Environments:** At their website, Welcoming America provides free toolkits, best practices reports, and webinars designed to help any organization or government lead an effort to build a welcoming community. Visit http://www.welcomingamerica.org/learn/resources to search for a resource.

Most of the cities featured in this book are part of the Welcoming America network: Boise, Idaho; Boston, Massachusetts; Buffalo, New York; Hartford, Connecticut; Houston, Texas; Los Angeles, California; Louisville, Kentucky; Multnomah County, Oregon; New York, New York; Philadelphia, Pennsylvania; and San José, California.

BUILDING COMMUNITY THROUGH CONVERSATIONS

As part of every interview for this book, I asked library staff: "What has the response from your community been to services and programs you provide to immigrants and refugees, or to statements the library has made regarding these initiatives?" Many of these interviews were conducted in the first half of 2017, as the new administration in Washington, D.C. was keying up the entire country, so if there had been a strong response from the community, that would have been the time to hear about it.

To a one, everyone said that the overwhelming majority of the response from their communities has been positive, and many were able to list all of the negative examples because there were so few. David Leonard at Boston Public Library was specific: "Our public message was almost universally praised . . . comments were appreciative, supportive, or positive. We did receive a small number of comments . . . from those who felt the Library was making a political statement. Some of those comments were clearly born out of the same feelings of disenfranchisement that surfaced during the recent presidential campaign, and while I will never condone one community attacking another, it is a reminder that there is deep concern being expressed on both sides of the political spectrum" (Leonard 2017).

Next door in Somerville, Glenn Ferdman saw a similar reaction: "We've had a lot of positive response to the [social media] posts: kudos from the board of trustees, lots of retweets of the resources tweet. [We did have] some negative comments on the Facebook post, some borderline racist comments, but the overwhelming majority of the comments were positive. [That said], no community is monolithic. You're always going to have some differences of opinion and this can, and tends to, be an emotional issue" (Ferdman 2017).

Outside the Northeast and off the coasts, the story was the same, though the details changed from place to place. A number of responders referenced being a "blue city/town in a red state," supporting the idea that even in largely conservative areas, there are places willing and able to take a more bipartisan perspective on topics like immigration. Libraries in these cities use that goodwill to bring in funds and other resources for services to newcomers.

Despite the largely positive response to many of the initiatives described in this book, every responder expressed a need for continued conversations; many of these quotes are in the chapters on accessibility and cultural programs, where we looked at some ways libraries have facilitated those discussions in other contexts. In the remainder of this chapter, you'll look at two programs explicitly designed to support deeper, potentially more challenging, conversations that can lead to deeper understanding of participants' own selves and of others.

What Happens When There's Trouble?

Nearly all of the libraries contacted for this book mentioned that there had been little negative feedback from the community on their work for immigrants and new Americans. At most, they amounted to cranky comments on social media posts or a brief heated exchange at a meeting. However, there is always the possibility of an incident at an event, or even a visit to the library by ICE officials.

The next two sections will look at a Cultural Literacy program and a Civic Lab; when developing these programs, staff anticipated that there may be heated interactions or challenges to the content. In one case, they prepared with copies of the library's behavior policy and a short script on how the topics may have been politicized, but are still within the library's scope. In the other, the very nature of the conversations are intended to touch on deeply held beliefs, and staff respond with researched, vetted, factual information.

Many resources are available for dealing with disruptive patrons or dangerous situations and for interacting with local officials; a few are listed here, but also contact your library, city, or county legal department for specifics on what you and your staff can and cannot do in situations like these. Another key thing to know is whether your city, county, or state has declared itself to be a "sanctuary" and precisely what the local government means by that; again, contact your local government legal department for guidance.

- "Libraries Respond: Immigrants, Refugees, and Asylum Seekers," an excellent list of resources from ALA, addresses interactions with officials for both libraries and your immigrant patrons: http://www.ala.org/advocacy/advocacy/diversity/libra ries-respond-immigrants-refugees-and-asylum-seekers

- "Raids & Enforcements: 9 Ways to Protect Yourself," from the Hartford Public Library, is directed toward individuals, but these tactics can also inform a library response: https://www.hplct.org/assets/uploads/files/Immigrant%20Rights%20 English.pdf

- "Dealing with Difficult Patrons: Incident Response and Documentation," by Nancy Relaford, is a good checklist of what to keep track of and how to respond in case of an incident: http://www.ala.org/llama/sites/ala.org.llama/files/content/conted /11-16-11_Relaford_Handout.pdf

- "Dealing with Difficult Patrons," a WebJunction webinar by Paul Signorelli and Maurice Coleman from 2010; their suggestions are still applicable, and WebJunction has kept the list of Related Resources updated: http://www.webjunction.org /events/webjunction/Dealing_with_Difficult_Patrons.html

(continued)

- *Library Security: Better Communication, Safer Facilities* by Steve Albrecht (ALA Editions, 2015).
- *The Black Belt Librarian: Real-World Safety & Security* by Warren Graham (ALA Editions 2012).
- Workshops at your state, regional, or national library conferences—this topic is a perennial one.

Cultural Literacy

Cedar Falls, Iowa, a town of 37,000 people, has always had some diversity due to students/professors at the University of Northern Iowa. In the past 15 years, an influx of immigrants and refugees that began with Latinos and Bosnians has expanded to include people from the Marshall Islands, Burma, and more. Sheryl McGovern, Director of the Cedar Falls Public Library, says, "In the past 11 years that I've been at the library, informal observation tells me we've gone from a patron base that was primarily Midwestern Caucasians to one that includes many more people of color, and people whose roots are not in the Midwest."

Over that same time, staff at the library have fielded increasing numbers of questions from patrons on how to get involved in the community and to "learn about global events on a local scale." Library users also wanted more interaction, expressing an interest in learning from other community members and organizations (McGovern 2017).

In response, the library developed the Cultural Literacy Series: monthly events to bring the community together around a specific theme. Erin Thompson, Technology Librarian, explains the purpose of the series: "The Cultural Literacy Series at CFPL aims to tie global issues to the Cedar Falls community both for informational purposes as well as to facilitate community involvement. We desire to start conversations, encourage learning, and inspire connections" (Thompson 2017). A secondary goal is to provide better access to facts that counteract fake or misleading information patrons receive.

The Cultural Literacy series kicked off in May 2017 with a discussion about refugees and immigrants in Cedar Valley by a panel of representatives from local organizations, many of whom were current or former refugees or undocumented immigrants. Subsequent programs have explored the Syrian refugee crisis, the concept of fair trade and artisan women in developing countries, Burmese immigrants and refugees (with EMBARC, the Ethnic Minorities of Burma Advocacy and Resource Center), and an inclusiveness panel on LGBTQ+ issues. During each one- to two-hour event, community residents or representatives from local organizations speak on the topic, then encourage engagement through questions and answers or discussion. Early audiences have averaged around 25 attendees, and the library anticipates growth as word spreads.

"Many of our patrons are thankful we started this series," says Sheryl, but staff are very aware that their patrons range across the political spectrum; staff also believe that the library is a neutral political environment, and that these conversations have a place there. In case of a disruptive patron, staff have a copy of library policies handy; to forestall complaints about the content, staff have also prepared statements along the lines of: "We can't be held responsible for the fact that these social and cultural issues have been politicized." Presenters, participants, and staff working on the series "believe our library shouldn't have a passive role in our community," adds Erin. "There's a renewed interest in learning about social and cultural issues and the library can provide access to programs in a neutral, free environment" (Thompson 2017).

Sheryl, who grew up in the area, notes, "It seems to me there will always be a need for a forum in which to discuss our changing cultural landscape. I would hate to assume that 'red' areas lack an understanding of the importance of diversity. I'm not sure our comfort level is directly linked to our politics, but there is a certain wariness of people who didn't grow up here." All the more reason for programs like the cultural literacy series, she says. "Yes, we may have some catching up to do, and the public library should step up to that responsibility, offering opportunities for education" (McGovern 2017).

Civic Lab

Like Cedar Falls, Skokie, Illinois, is a Midwestern town that has seen increasing numbers of culturally diverse newcomers in recent years, continuing a decades-long trend of immigration to Skokie that began after World War II. In the winter of 2015, Skokie Public Library participated in a community-wide program called "Voices of Race," a response to the renewed awareness of violence toward persons of color by police. Many of the library's activities and programs were very well attended, especially discussions of personal experiences with racial prejudice and a gallery wall where patrons and staff shared images and words around personal identity. "The level of interest and participation in 'Voices of Race' signaled to those of us on the programming team that our community had an as-yet-untapped interest in exploring conversations and topics related to race and identity," says Amy Koester, Youth and Family Program Supervisor at Skokie, as well as topics raised during the 2016 presidential election and other current events (Koester 2017).

In August 2016, the library ran a pilot program—the "Civic Lab Boutique"—offering information and thought-provoking activities to support dialogue on six issues affecting the Skokie community: Black Lives Matter, climate change, immigration, income inequality, LGBTQQI issues, and reproductive justice. Based on feedback from the pilot and patron requests after the 2016 presidential election, the library restructured and fully implemented the program.

The Skokie Public Library Civic Lab is a series of pop-up installations and large events that facilitate exploration of and discussion on topics affecting the community and the nation, based on vetted information. A small multidepartment team serves as curators of the Civic Lab; they look at upcoming library programs, topics in the news, and topics from previous pop-ups and community interactions to identify possible themes. One team member acts as lead for each topic, coordinating staff, scheduling one or two pop-up sessions, creating resource handouts, curating browsing collections of books and digital media, and developing related activities.

The most successful pop-ups often come from the personal interests of staff. A staff member's participation in the protests at Standing Rock in November 2016 translated into a robust pop-up that gave participants a different perspective than the voices they heard during news casts. Similarly, a staff member's interest in CRISPR (genome editing technology) led to conversations about medical technology and ethics. "Our resources are better curated, and our conversations more robust, when we engage with expertise and experience along with information," adds Amy.

During a one- to two-hour pop-up, patrons ask questions, read and write responses to topic prompts on sticky notes in an asynchronous conversation, and engage in discussion with facilitators. Costs are minimal: 12 wooden crates that serve as flexible furniture, a program banner and stand, and a mobile iPad display; ongoing costs are for printing and food.

To complement the pop-ups, the library has hosted three 8-hour community-building programs in a series called "Together at the Table." Attendees of every age and background filled out name tags, enjoyed baked treats, and were introduced to fellow community members. Staff chose prompts from "The 36 Questions That Lead to Love" (Katz 2015) as conversation starters to help strangers connect on a human level. The first event on Martin Luther King Day 2017 was incredibly successful, with rich discussions taking place across families, generations, and communities; a second event in June took place during Ramadan, with snacks and dates to break the fast after sundown.

Beyond strong attendance numbers and positive feedback, Amy's favorite outcome is a quote from a participant at a "How does the Supreme Court work?" pop-up. After a discussion about civic engagement, the participant said, "You need to have good information in order to make up your own mind. If you have bad information, someone else is making up your mind for you." Amy adds, "If one of our goals is to ensure that participants have access to reputable information that helps them better recognize, understand, and reflect on what's going on in the community and the world, this quote helps us to see that we're having some success."

Although the Civic Lab is intended to encourage conversations, says Amy, "It's important to recognize that both active and passive elements have value and audience. Not every person wants to engage in a discussion about free speech and hate speech if they haven't had time and space for personal reflection first, and so it's integral to have elements that inspire both personal reflection and larger conversation. There's a time, place, and audience for both" (Koester 2017).

A NETWORK OF TRUST

When a library puts itself at the center of an effort to build community around the needs of immigrants and refugees, exceptional things can happen. As a testament to this, let's end this chapter with a description of the "networks of trust" built by and centered on the Hartford Public Library, as described on their website. Visit http://www.hplct.org/library-services /immigration-citizenship/community-civic-participation to follow the links mentioned in the text.

Building Networks of Trust

In October 2010, Hartford Public Library received a three-year National Leadership Grant from the federal Institute of Museum and Library Services to promote immigrant civic involvement. Several strategies have been implemented, all rooted in the concept of *building networks of trusting relationships* between immigrants and the receiving community. As a demonstration project, this initiative is being thoroughly documented on this website so that the model may be replicated by other cities in the future . . .

Strategy 1: Recruit and train volunteers to serve as Cultural Navigators. These mentors are integral to easing the transition of newly arrived immigrants into their home city, Hartford. The Cultural Navigator (CN) Program is designed to recruit and train volunteers to help guide new arrival immigrants as they adjust to living in Hartford. [The Cultural Navigator program is described in Chapter 2.]

Strategy 2: Build coalitions among key stakeholders. The Immigrant Advisory Group (IAG) serves as a city-wide vehicle for stakeholders to communicate current

---

(continued)

immigration issues and share best practices with each other. It is also a forum for participants to learn about immigrant cultures and experiences. [This was the group that became the city Commission on Refugee and Immigrant Affairs.]

Strategy 3: Engage immigrants and the receiving community in Community Dialogues on topics of mutual concern. There are various approaches to this, but all lead to a plan of action. Hartford Public Library has piloted two approaches: City Wide and Neighborhood.

Strategy 4: Bridge cultures through facilitated book group discussions and films that portray the immigrant experience and its often-complex cross-cultural dynamics.

Strategy 5: Foster the value that regardless of where you come from, Hartford welcomes you and We Belong Here Hartford.

SOURCE: https://www.hplct.org/library-services/immigration-citizenship/community-civic-participation

SUMMING UP

One of the great strengths of libraries is their reputation for being "free to all," for every definition of both "free" and "all."

"Free" in terms of cost, free in terms of accessible, and free in terms of constitutional and legal freedoms "with the full rights of U.S. residents."

"All" in that everyone and anyone is permitted to walk in the doors, watch a video, read a book, listen to music, search a database, and attend a program. There may be restrictions on who can take home materials, but anyone can come inside.

As this free, neutral space, libraries are perfectly situated to help build community through outreach, partnerships, and conversations. Getting out into the community to find users and not-yet-users and invite them in is even more crucial for immigrant populations—who may not be familiar with the concepts behind U.S.-style public libraries—than it is for U.S.-born residents. Reaching out to the organizations that serve immigrant populations and making use of their referral networks can extend the reach of the library tenfold. Inviting both newcomers and their receiving community neighbors in for honest, respectful conversations can cement the bonds that begin during lighthearted events like a Family Storytelling Night.

The last chapter will look at ways to expand services, from getting the word out to finding the funding.

8

◆ ◆ ◆

EXPANDING SERVICES

When considering serving immigrants and new Americans, the first thing to remember is: you're already doing something. Even if you don't have a single program or service that says "ESL" or "for immigrants," you are serving these populations through your existing work. This chapter addresses how to take whatever your library is already doing and expand on it:

- By attracting more participants from newcomer communities
- By gathering data and measuring outcomes to justify services
- By finding sources of funding to support the work and maximize what you have

Historically, these are areas that challenge many libraries—talking up their services, quantifying impact, and asking for money—but together they form a sequence that can systematically increase your ability to provide the services we've discussed in this book. When you bring in more users and measure how what you're doing positively affects their lives, you can attract larger and larger funding sources that allow you to bring in more users, and the virtuous cycle continues.

PROMOTION AND MARKETING

Although this book has already covered the incidental promotion that happens as a result of outreach and partnership building, this section focuses on specific efforts to get the word out, from the most successful to the most traditional.

There's a frustrating fact about library promotion, summed up by an interviewee: "It's shocking but true that some librarians believe they can put a flyer up and wait for something to happen. Or, more scary [sic], they put a flyer up and nothing happens and the librarians say, 'Oh, obviously people in this community aren't interested in this program,' or 'I guess that people don't need to work on their English around here!' Just based on sticking up little flyers. That's a pet peeve of mine. I'm not suggesting that everyone needs to wake up, text message, and blur that line between their professional life and their work life, but I think there's a happy medium there." In this chapter, you'll explore ways to find the happy medium.

Word of Mouth Is Everything

I repeat: word of mouth is **everything**.

Nearly to a one, every library consulted for this project said that word of mouth is the single best way to get folks from immigrant and refugee populations (or other marginalized groups) into the library for programs and services. The "who" and the "how" might vary from library to library, but in the end, it is personal recommendations to individuals that bring them in. Which is to say, don't spend a fortune on slick marketing materials and promotional spots before you have worked every length of your community contact web.

MyTesha Tates, Community Engagement Manager at Houston Public Library, spells it out: "Much of our marketing has been via word of mouth and flyers—word gets around!" (Tates 2016).

"These are relationship-based communities," explains Maddy Ildefonso, Senior Librarian in the Office of Enrichment and Empowerment at the Los Angeles Public Library. "People are generally likely to take information they get from a family member or a friend who went to the classes. [A program might] start off slow and you'd think, Oh my gosh, all these resources and only four people, five people show. Then suddenly you have 20 people in your class because their friends told their friends, and that's how it usually unfolds" (Ildefonso 2017).

One likely reason for the singular success of word-of-mouth promotion is that many newcomers may view any governmental agency—even the library—with suspicion, either because the governments in their countries of origin were ineffectual or antagonistic, or due to tensions about their immigration status. Glenn Ferdman, Director of Somerville Public Library, opined, "Offering programs to undocumented persons is a particular challenge because we're part of the city government, and in some people's minds, that equates us with the police or ICE. That can create a barrier to entry for some people, in spite of the fact that we're a sanctuary city. . . . In spite of the fact that the library is often seen as very friendly, non-judgmental, free and open to everyone . . . in the current [political] climate, it still represents a challenge because it's an environment of fear" (Ferdman 2017).

Word of mouth is a challenge, but for a new or experimental program— or some long-term "forgotten" programs—there may be no budget for marketing and promotion. Asking current patrons, program participants, and "library evangelists" in the community to talk up programs and services to friends and family is the most direct way to reach an intended audience. In addition, showing the potential of a program through wildly successful word-of-mouth promotion can establish that effort as a priority in the eyes of library or government administrators and lead to broader support.

After more than two years in the Department of Lifelong Learning, Alicia Moguel of Los Angeles Public Library asked, "If this is something that's been institutionalized in our library system, why isn't there more effort to promote these programs? It's been a successful program, primarily by word of mouth and the work that the librarians have done in the community. Now we are finally getting to do a library system- and city-wide scale promotion through a professional marketing campaign; we are currently working with an outside agency and our PR department [on this campaign]" (Moguel 2017).

The previous chapter discussed library outreach to individuals and organizations as a part of a community-building effort. In this section, let's address the community's outreach to itself, especially via 21st-century technologies.

Library Ambassadors

Unlike "social media campaigns" or customer relationship efforts, word of mouth involves finding the social "connectors" of your community and encouraging them to promote the library everywhere they go. In his book *The Tipping Point,* Malcolm Gladwell identifies three types of communicators who make an idea spread:

- **Connectors** know and keep in touch with many people.
- **Movers** are information specialists and masters at linking efforts.
- **Salesmen** build rapport and are "socially contagious" people themselves (Gladwell 2000).

For our discussion, the Connectors are the folks to find: the people (like Sophie Maier and her mother Donna in Louisville or Moina Noor in Norwalk) who seem to know *everyone* and can contact hundreds of people with a single post or email. You may not have an official Library Ambassadors program—though some libraries do—but knowing who your ambassadors are and making sure they have current information is a key to these efforts. Because they also tend to be library power users, they may already scoop up flyers and calendars every time they come in; cultivate them by actively mentioning new initiatives or chatting about wanting to expand your library's reach into immigrant and refugee communities.

On that note, if you're a library administrator or supervisor, encourage your staff to take time to chit-chat with patrons. These warm, comfortable connections are a foundation in being a friendly, accessible library, as discussed in Chapter 2 and seen in the example from Norwalk in Chapter 7. Staff should be mindful of the needs of other patrons and their duties, of course, but try to support them in having opportunities for these personal interactions.

Occasionally, your ambassadors will approach you, as Cathy Piantigini, Deputy Director of Somerville Public Library, discovered. "Just last week, a patron emailed us who was part of the Somerville Family Learning Collaborative," who was updating the collaborative's ESL class information along with a counterpart at another organization. "She noticed that she had current information that the library didn't have, and she sent us the updated document. [The library] is on everyone's radar right now; not only are we providing information, but other folks are reaching out to us and sharing their updated information so we have it too" (Piantigini 2017).

Tech Tools for Word of Mouth

Social media and mobile devices: some folks live on them, some loathe them, but their potential as word-of-mouth promotion tools cannot be denied. Even though Facebook isn't as effective as it once was—new algorithms often bury posts so that only a fraction of followers see them—it can still be an effective tool for the right audience.

Sophie Maier is typical in her mixed feelings about social media: "I use Facebook a lot, and I hate it. I don't want to be on Facebook, but a lot of the immigrant groups I work with, either the organizations or the individuals, use FB a lot and that's their preferred method [of contact]. It is great that once you get folks in those individual communities sharing information, that's the most useful of all" (Maier 2017).

Twitter and other social platforms seem to be less universal, but if you learn that a particular community you're trying to reach has a favorite, it only makes sense to be using it too. For a basic introduction to library social media, read David Lee King's book *Face2Face: Using Facebook, Twitter, and Other Social Media Tools to Create Great Customer Connections.*

A more targeted approach, but one that requires more trust for participants and maintenance of contact information, are text message or email "blasts." These instant reminders go directly to recipients and are much more likely to be seen, but require the effort to collect and regularly update that list of contacts to be effective.

Sophie admits that she texts a lot: "I'm really annoying the night before a program. I have a big list of contacts and I'll send out a text message blast in the early morning on Saturdays [before the English Conversation Club or Cultural Showcase] to remind folks" (Maier 2017).

In many places outside the United States, WhatsApp has replaced standard text messaging as a preferred mode of contact. Through the WhatsApp app or web interface, a sender can instantly message, call, or share files using the device's Internet connection rather than using standard phone calls or text messages; this is especially important in places where cellular connections are monitored, because it's not as easy to discern what's going across an Internet connection. Messages can be sent to individuals or groups up to 256 people with a single tap, making these "blasts" as simple as email.

In Norwalk, library trustee and "ambassador" Moina Noor uses WhatsApp to reach the multinational community of her mosque. "For the family storytelling night, Vicki gave me all these flyers and of course I put them around and they had the emails, but . . . I knew that 3 to 4 days before, I was going to have to go to my WhatsApp group and start sending messages like, 'We need to go! It'll be a fun evening with your kids and there'll be free pizza!'"

Moina embraces this work with open arms. "I have become—both because of my role [as board member] at the library and because I love the library—I've become the library ambassador at my mosque. Sometimes,

I think that having those point people is what you need in marketing, kind of in that grassroots marketing kind of way. I did put [the family storytelling night] on our Facebook group, I did all the things I needed to do" (Noor 2017).

Traditional Marketing

Word of mouth in person and via technology are, by far, the most effective ways to reach newcomer residents. There is still value, however, in more traditional communication tools, especially in very well-established communities with multigenerational waves of immigrants who speak the same language.

One challenge to marketing directly to immigrants in languages other than English is translation, as we saw in Chapter 2 on the sections on signage and websites. If you have library staff fluent in the target languages and willing to translate flyer after flyer, the process is as straightforward as the same efforts in English. If not, community volunteers or professional translation services will be much more accurate than Google Translate and similar machine-based tools. For these reasons, most libraries limit translation to a few "evergreen" items like informational flyers or brochures or materials promoting large events likely to be of interest to newcomers. Similarly, press releases to non-English broadcast, print, and online media can be sent in English, but are then left to be translated by the media outfit and may not have the nuanced message of your original document.

Another hurdle is finding relevant media to send promotional materials to, as the number of local broadcasts and news media decreases and moves online or to national networks. In well-established immigrant communities, there may be local television stations, public access television programs, radio stations, newspapers, circulars, or magazines, but probably not for the new group of refugees who have just been resettled. Check business, marketing, and similar databases that your library, network, or consortium subscribes to for lists of stations in your area. It's more likely that there are online resources in the hundreds of languages spoken in a typical metro area, but there again we run into issues of literacy in the native language and digital skills.

As with materials in other languages, the best way to know what languages to focus on and how to reach those media outlets is to ask the people you're trying to reach. Find out where and how they get their local news (that isn't from friends and family), and search for contacts for those organizations. Stop into small markets or restaurants and note what's sitting on print media racks, playing over the store's loudspeakers, or visible on a corner television. Develop connections with other organizations or individuals who put on large events—cultural organizations, music promoters, dance school owners—and find out where they promote their shows. Relying on your community partners will not just help you reach individuals, but can connect you to a more extensive communication network.

MAKING THE CASE

In today's atmosphere of user research, data-driven decisions, and outcomes measurement, anecdotal justifications for programs and services hold less and less weight. Researching your service populations as part of developing programs and quantitatively measuring both outputs (like circulation numbers and program attendance) and outcomes can produce charts and graphs that are more likely to convince funding agencies to commit dollars and municipal administrators to commit resources.

Collecting Data

Collecting demographic data (about age, sex, education level, income level, ethnicity, country of origin) about your community is a first step to producing quality programs for newcomers in your area; knowing new or growing cultural and language groups can help identify the specific resources you'll need to support those services. National, state, and city/county censuses can provide general data, but may not be granular enough to identify needs for the area surrounding a neighborhood library. Sources for extremely local information include:

- City or county neighborhood development departments and offices of immigrant affairs
- Community Development Corporations (CDCs), who may or may not be part of a government agency
- Organizations working with newcomer populations, especially refugee resettlement and health agencies
- Business demographic databases
- Other city/county reports on "service deserts" and other municipal service priorities
- For library-wide strategic planning efforts, it may make sense to commission a detailed analysis from a private firm

As part of this data-driven approach, some municipal governments are changing the way they plan city buildings and services. As mentioned at the end of Chapter 6, the city of Boise has begun using a health impact assessment as part of the process of constructing new city buildings. Sarah Kelley-Chase of the Bown Crossing location of the Boise Public Library describes the assessment: "It's a fairly new process that looks at how physically placing a building affects the immediate community [along] seven aspects of health: physical, social, economic, environmental, intellectual, emotional, and spiritual. With that, the group that helped get the study going for us did a lot of demographic work. About 40% of our population here is either under 18 or over 65, so [the study revealed] a lot of really interesting opportunities for inter-generational programming. Economically, this side of town tends to have a higher income overall **but** we're in a pocket that is right next to apartments, rentals, students, retirees, and refugees less than a mile away. There's an elementary school that's a little over a mile away called White Pine, that has a large percentage of students for whom English is not their first language" (Kelley-Chase 2017). To see the results of the Library! at Bown Crossing health impact survey, visit http://www.boi sepubliclibrary.org/media/9616/BownLibrary-Boise-HIA-DRAFT.pdf.

For more about health impact assessments for non-health related services, visit the Center for Disease Control HIA information page at http://www.cdc.gov/healthyplaces/hia.htm or the American Public Health Association's *Health in All Policies* fact sheet at https://www.apha.org/~ /media/files/pdf/factsheets/health_inall_policies_guide_169pages.ashx

Outcomes Measurement

Ask a public librarian about outcomes measurement and you're likely to get a lukewarm response. Measuring outcomes can be a vital step in justifying library programs and services, but it can be overwhelming. As Sophie of Louisville says, "Sadly, I'm not a quantitative person . . . I've always been anecdotal and I think the only reason that we're getting recognition/acknowledgement is that there are enough anecdotes now. If there's anything I regret, it's that I never learned how to be a storyteller with numbers that help when it comes time to asking for money or additional staff support" (Maier 2017). When creating or expanding services, especially to a focused group like new Americans, these measurements are critical to getting support of funds and resources.

Before looking at ways to measure outcomes, let's review what we're talking about. In a *Library Journal* article from 2015, Samantha Becker,

Principal Research Scientist of the Impact Survey, defined these measurement terms (Becker 2015):

- **Indicator:** a measure that something has happened
- **Input:** amount of time, money, equipment, work going into a program or service; measured directly
- **Output:** numbers coming out of a program or service; measured directly
- **Outcome:** amount of change due to a program or service: measured indirectly
- **Logic model:** a linear structure for thinking about program/service indicators, inputs, outputs, and outcomes
- **Theory of change model:** a list of "so that" statements linking a program idea to a desired or possible outcome

Inputs and outputs are relatively straightforward for libraries to keep track of: how many staff worked for how many hours on a project, how many dollars were spent to support it, how many people attended, or how many materials were distributed and circulated. Library staff have also incorporated simple surveys for immediate feedback into their programs for years and are adept at collecting those stories that Sophie mentioned.

What many funding agencies and municipal oversight officers are looking for now are **outcomes**: the mid- to long-term impact of an effort on the people it touches. Three initiatives are working nationally to help libraries track and analyze outcomes (Koerber 2017):

Project Outcome: Project Outcome was the result of work initiated by PLA's Performance Measurement Task Force, established in 2013 by then-PLA president Carolyn Anthony. By providing a set of standardized, easy-to-use outcome surveys and the ability to aggregate the results, Project Outcome removes a major barrier to this kind of measurement: the amount of work it takes to design useful surveys. Project Outcome encourages libraries to distribute surveys on paper or online both immediately after a program and as a follow-up a few weeks later. Most of the questions use a rating scale, but open-ended questions at the end of the survey are most useful for both positive and change-inducing feedback. Libraries enter the paper survey responses into the Project Outcome platform—online forms feed directly to the platform's databases—and the project's staff provide support in interpreting and applying the results to advocacy efforts.

Impact Survey: In 2009, the University of Washington's iSchool developed and distributed a survey to try and determine the impact of library technology on patrons, appropriately titled the U.S. Impact Survey. After the national project was complete, libraries asked to use the survey locally. In response, the researchers developed the Impact Survey: "a tool to let libraries run technology surveys on their own schedule; at the conclusion of the survey, the library receives easy-to-share, automatically generated reports such as customized presentation slides, handouts, and news article templates" (Koerber 2017). Impact Survey researchers are also available to help library staff use this data internally for planning needs and externally to increase support.

Edge Initiative: In contrast to these two projects, the Edge Initiative from the Urban Libraries Council encourages libraries to assess their technology itself. Using an online tool, libraries identify strengths, gaps, and areas of improvement for technology infrastructure and services by measuring against 11 standardized benchmarks. With their Edge results, libraries can create a plan to strengthen technology services and seek out community partnerships.

Though these initiatives aren't solely directed at services to immigrants and new Americans, those groups are part of the community that a library serves and can be included in efforts to measure outcomes across all of a library's programs and services. Both Project Outcome and the Impact Survey intend to increase the number of surveys available in languages other than English, and the service areas measured by both projects closely match the chapter topics of this book: civic/community engagement (citizenship and cultural programs), economic development and job skills (workforce development), education/lifelong learning and early childhood literacy (ESOL and citizenship), and technology and digital learning (accessibility and workforce development).

As an example of both outputs and outcomes in action, consider some of the measures from the Civic Labs at Skokie Public Library. Amy Koester of Skokie describes what they record: "We've been documenting an assortment of things for the Civic Lab. In terms of outputs, we'll keep track of how many people participate in each pop-up, how many people take handouts or other related materials, how many people participate in a voting prompt as part of the pop-up, etc. In terms of outcomes, we're often looking at the qualitative data we collect during the pop-ups. How many people shared indicators of having learned something or considering something they hadn't thought about before as a result of the pop-up? Do people feel compelled to learn more as a result of participating in a pop-up and, more specifically, a conversation with a staff member or another participant? Do participants have a greater sense of the mission of the library as it pertains to civic engagement and information literacy as a result of participating in the Civic Lab? We've found that while upwards of 30% of participants display indicators of intending to learn more after participating in the Civic Lab (which, frankly, we consider to be a high rate of intended follow-through, especially since many patrons stumble on the Civic Lab serendipitously rather than plan to attend), over 80% express that they've learned something as a result of participating" (Koester 2017).

FUNDING

Since the global financial crisis of 2008, libraries have seen budgets slashed, budget votes knocked down, and a decrease in overall availability of grant funds. It remains to be seen what effect the presidential administration that took control in 2017 will have on the viability of many long-time funding sources, but at the time of this writing, the prospects appear dim but not dire. (One question that remains unanswered is the promise by then-candidate Donald Trump of financial consequences for "sanctuary cities" described in Chapter 1.)

Even in the current environment, there are resources that can help expand services to newcomers, though they may take a bit more creativity and effort to find. Also, as we've discussed in a few earlier sections, there are ways to extend existing resources through "free help," organizational partnership networks, and philanthropy.

One thing to consider when applying for funding is how changes in national policy toward immigrants might alter what kind of programs you can—or should—offer. The Hartford Foundation for Public Giving had awarded funds to the Hartford Public Library for outreach to DACA applicants, but the library chose to hold off on implementing the program given the uncertain future of the DACA initiative. Homa explains, "We have funding to increase our legal capacity to submit those legal applications, but we decided not to because we don't know what is going to go on. I mean, if we submit these applications, their names are going to be [officially recorded], and so we pulled back from that and instead re-focused on encouraging people who have green cards to renew their green cards or apply for citizenship" (Naficy 2017).

Increased Library and Municipal Resources

As libraries commit to serving immigrants and new Americans as an institutional priority (Chapter 2), they and their municipality must support that commitment by reallocating resources and moving budgets around. Sometimes it means providing for staff (re)training and expanding existing services (also Chapter 2), or it might necessitate adding programs to serve these populations (Chapters 3 through 6). Whatever the need, whether it's staff time, line-item budgets, or support from other departments, a library and its governing body should do what it can to help their initiatives to newcomers succeed.

In previous chapters, you saw the ways in which libraries have been able to create these programs and services on low or no budgets, using volunteer "helpers" and donated time and services from professionals, and minimal marketing. However, we've also seen how the application of resources, even just in terms of paid staff time, can boost already successful programs to new levels of reach. Using the data and measurements discussed earlier, you can make the case for your library or city government to shift resources according to demonstrated needs and outcomes.

There are many resources in print and online for advocating for your library—here are a couple to kick-start your search:

- "Advocacy Tips from a Library Pro" by Judy Drescher at the PLA *Turning the Page* blog, http://www.ala.org/pla/education/turningthepage/librarypro
- *The Advocacy Action Plan Workbook* from the ALA Advocacy Institute, http://www.ala.org/advocacy/sites/ala.org.advocacy/files/content/advleg/advocacyinstitute/Advocacy%20Action%20Plan%20-%20revised%2001-09.pdf
- "How to Advocate for Your Library Through [Digital] Storytelling" by Ginny Mies at TechSoup, http://www.techsoupforlibraries.org/blog/how-to-advocate-for-your-library-through-storytelling
- "15 Ways to Harness the Power of Nonprofit Storytelling for Advocacy" by Joe Fuld for the Nonprofit Technology Network, http://www.nten.org/article/15-ways-harness-power-nonprofit-storytelling-advocacy/

Local Sources

For many libraries in this book, local philanthropy is a cornerstone of the funding they receive for programs. Sheryl McGovern, Director of Cedar Falls, stresses the importance of these resources to the success of her library's work: "We are very blessed. We do have an active and supportive Friends group. They raise funds through memberships, and a small, used book store within the library. We also have funds in the Cedar Falls Community Foundation that allows us about $100,000 annually for special projects, building enhancements, and programming. We do ask for sponsorships for some programs, too, and have had great support from local businesses. We could not be the sort of library we are without these funding sources" (McGovern 2017).

In Hartford, Homa finds the same generosity from the Hartford Foundation for Public Giving. The Career Pathways project is funded by the foundation, along with projects from eight other organizations, all designed along the guidelines of collective impact. Representatives from the nine projects meet quarterly to exchange ideas, says Homa. "They're looking for all of our organizations to work together for collective impact to help people who are chronically unemployed or constantly unemployed. We're the only ones focused on immigrants in this collaboration" (Naficy 2017).

Resources like Foundation Directory or GrantWatch do include locally focused philanthropists, but may be hard to navigate. There are some additional tools to find funders looking to help organizations in your state or local area:

- Wells Fargo Bank has a search engine for private foundations who work with their philanthropic services unit at http://www.wellsfargo.com/private-foundations.
- The Grantsmanship Center charges a fee for most of its content, but you can access the Top 10 Grantmaking Foundations and other information by state for free. Visit this page and scroll down to the map to get the list for your state: http://www.tgci.com/funding-sources.
- *The Almanac of American Philanthropy* (Compact Edition or Full Edition) by Karl Zinsmeister. The Philanthropy Roundtable, Washington D.C., annual.

Grants

After library budgets and local giving, grants were the single biggest source for funding for implementing the projects described in earlier chapters. Grant applications do require effort to prepare, but as ways to kick-start a pilot project to prove its success, they are usually worth it.

Two facts emerged from the research for this book: 1) there are thousands of potential grant sources at the city, state, and national level; and

2) although there are a limited number specifically designated for immigrants, many apply to a particular *type* of program for which the library can determine the intended audience. For instance, rather than seeking a grant that is aimed at improving workforce readiness of immigrants, apply for a general workforce development grant and note that your project's intended participants are a new and growing population who speak a particular language.

If your library provides access to Foundation Directory or Grantwatch, or you have a workspace in Grants.gov, you can search thousands of grants in a single sitting. Look for grants that offer funding for:

- Services to immigrants or refugees
- Library innovation or programming
- Technology-driven areas like website redesigns or equitable access to mobile devices
- Small business initiatives
- Workforce development (Workforce Innovation and Opportunity Act [WOIA]–related grants)
- Social programs grants
- Support for school-aged children—as we saw in the section on family literacy, supporting children can also support their caregivers
- Cultural grants
- Arts and literature grants
- Additional grant suggestions from ALA at http://www.ala.org/tools/research/larks/grants

Another tip is to "multitask" your grant: use a grant to create or support a program that can serve all of your users and also provide a boost for specific populations. For instance, you can apply for an arts grant intended to support literature discussions, and design your program to include discussions in both English and additional high-impact languages. In a technology grant to overhaul the library website, earmark a portion of it for usability improvements and translation services. Don't let the perfect be the enemy of the good—get creative in the vision for your program to expand the possible sources for support.

All of this said, let's look at a few grants targeted for services to immigrants to know what might be available.

Statewide Grants at the Fresno County Public Library

In 2017, Fresno County Public Library received two grants to support its programs for immigrants: a grant from the California Center for the Book on Community Conversations about Immigration, and a California Humanities Library Innovation Lab grant to explore new ways of engaging California's immigrant communities. Both grants were used to fund parts of the "Coming to California" cultural sharing series described in Chapter 6, with the Center for the Book grant covering the earlier parts of the series and the California Humanities grant supporting the story jam that was the series finale, as well as additional programs.

Although the grants themselves are geared toward topics around immigration, the funding that supports them comes from multiple organizations, all of which are much broader fundraising efforts. California Center for the Book receives its support as part of the national network of Centers for the Book coordinated by the Library of Congress and from Institute for Museum and Library Services (IMLS) via the California Library Association. California Humanities is an independent nonprofit organization that directly raises money for its programs from foundations, corporations, government agencies, and individuals and is a partner of the National Endowment for the Humanities. For more information about both grants, visit the California Center for the Book (http://calbook.org /programs/californians-community-conversations-about-immigration) and California Humanities (http://calhum.org/programs-initiatives/pro grams/library-innovation-lab) websites.

The American Dream Literacy Initiative

A program of grants administered by ALA's Office for Diversity, Literacy, and Outreach Services, the American Dream Literacy Initiative seeks to strengthen library-based adult literacy programs. Through these grants, libraries have added to their print and digital ESL collections; increased computer access and training; provided job training; hold literacy, education, and citizenship classes; and increased community awareness of services to immigrants and new Americans. ALA also asks that libraries document their process and make sure that their programs are replicable at libraries with a variety of resources available.

The Schaumburg Township District Library was a two-time recipient of The American Dream grant and used the funds to purchase materials and increase the number of classes to help area immigrants. Says Helen Stewart, Literacy Coordinator at Schaumburg, "We were able to provide citizenship classes at the Hoffman Estates and Hanover Park branches, in addition to the Central Library . . . We also expanded the ESL collection at both branches." A key part of their grant application was the data that Schaumburg, a suburb northwest of Chicago, has an extremely diverse population with more than 85 different languages spoken (Stewart 2017).

Extending Your Resources

In some ways, many of these suggestions were addressed in previous chapters, but let's quickly review ways to use the resources you have to reach a wider audience:

- Volunteers, through formal programs or informally as "helpers"
- Pro bono donations of skills/equipment/time from professionals in related fields
- Partnerships with local organizations, 1:1 or in larger networks
- Restructuring existing programs and services to be more accessible to newcomers
- Re-examining your outreach efforts and community connections to find new lines of support
- Including considerations for multiple languages and cultural awareness in staff training and library-wide improvement initiatives

CONCLUSION

Over the past century, libraries have emerged as a central point for immigrants to enter the greater civic life of their new communities, whether through improving their English, becoming citizens, developing their workforce skills, sharing their cultures, or contributing to a larger community conversation. As we begin the next century with high levels of uncertainty about the status and attitude toward newcomers to this country, it's more imperative than ever for libraries to remain these open, supportive, and welcoming places. I hope that these examples from dozens of libraries have inspired you to begin or expand your services to these vital new residents, celebrating the benefits of a diverse community and helping newcomers integrate more fully into local life.

As a final thought, reconsider Mary Jean Jakubowski's thoughts that opened Chapter 2: "The best advice is to start small . . . Identify one or two things the library can do to support the transition process . . . Simple steps like hanging welcome signage in native languages, ensuring staff is mindful and respectful of cultural customs, and meeting with members of your local immigrant and refugee community are all important components in making immigrants and refugees feel comfortable." Provide a space that newcomers feel welcome in, and let the rest follow (Jakubowski 2016).

REFERENCES

Addington, Renee. Personal communication with the author, August 2017. Branch Librarian, Library! at Bown Crossing, Boise Public Library.

Aldermen of the City of Somerville. 1989. *Somerville Sanctuary City Resolution*, Board of Aldermen, City of Somerville, May 11, 1989. Accessed November 11, 2017. http://www.somervillema.gov/sites/default/files/1989-sanctuary-city-resolution.pdf

Aldermen of the City of Somerville. 2016. *Reaffirming Somerville as a Sanctuary/Trust Act City*, Board of Aldermen, City of Somerville, December 8, 2016. Accessed November 11, 2017. http://www.somervillema.gov/sites/default/files/2016-sanctuary-city-resolution.pdf

ALL Access in the Libraries, Rhode Island. n.d. About page. Accessed November 12, 2017. http://allaccessri.org/about/

Allen-Hart, Joan. 2011. "Legal Reference vs. Legal Advice." In *Locating the Law: a Handbook for Non-Law Librarians*, 5th ed, rev., edited by June Kim, 46–53. Southern California Association of Law Libraries. Creative Commons license A-NC-ND. Accessed November 12, 2017. http://scallnet.org/wp-content/uploads/2016/03/ch4.pdf

Anonymous patron comment, via Joan Vestal. Personal communication with the author, August 2017. Information Services Librarian (retired), Boise Public Library.

Aurora Public Library. n.d. Mission Statement page. Accessed November 12, 2017. http://www.aurorapubliclibrary.org/mission-statement/

Baanante, Sharon. n.d. "Our Story" at the Love ALL Project. Accessed November 12, 2017. http://loveallproject.org/#our_story

Baanante, Sharon. Personal communication with the author, August 2017. Founder, Love ALL Project.

Baker, Diane. Personal communication with the author, July 2016. Business Management Director and NWC Project Manager, Carson City Library.

Batalova, Jeanne, Michael Fix, and James D. Bachmeier. 2016. *Untapped Talent: The Costs of Brain Waste among Highly Skilled Immigrants in the United States*. Washington, DC: Migration Policy Institute, New American Economy, and World Education Services.

Becker, Samantha. 2015. "Outcomes, Impacts, and Indicators." *Library Journal*, September 18, 2015. Accessed September 29, 2017. http://lj.libraryjournal.com /2015/09/managing-libraries/outcomes-impacts-and-indicators/

Boise Public Library. n.d. "Sohbat with Rumi" event description. Accessed November 12, 2017. http://www.boisepubliclibrary.org/classes-events/online -calendar/?trumbaEmbed=view%3Devent%26eventid%3D125180247

Boston Public Library. 2014. Bibliocycle-tagged entries in Press Blog. Accessed November 12, 2017. http://www.bpl.org/press/tag/bibliocycle/

Bourne, Jill. Personal communication with the author, June–July 2017. Director, San José Public Library.

Buffalo & Erie County Public Library Knight News Challenge proposal, submitted April 2016. *Knight News Challenge proposal—"The Community Welcomes You Project:" Libraries as an integral part of the immigrant and refugee assimilation process into the community*. Submitted April 2016. Downloaded May 2016, no longer available online.

California Senate Bill 54 (SB-54). 2016. Accessed September 29, 2017. https://leginfo .legislature.ca.gov/faces/billNavClient.xhtml?bill_id=201720180SB54

Chant, Ian. 2015. "Louisville Libraries Help Train Local Talent for Tech Jobs," *Library Journal*, April 17, 2015. Accessed December 2, 2017. http://lj.library journal.com/2015/04/technology/louisville-libraries-help-train-local-talent -for-tech-jobs/

City of Somerville. n.d. "About SomerViva." Accessed November 12, 2017. http:// www.somervillema.gov/somerviva

Cunningham, Kate. Interview by the author, April 10, 2017. English Conversation Club helper, Iroquois Branch, Louisville Free Public Library.

Curtatone, Joseph A. 2014. *Executive Policy for Responding to ICE Detainers*. Mayor Joseph A. Curtatone, May 22, 2014. Accessed November 11, 2017. http://www.somervillema.gov/sites/default/files/2014-ice-executive -order.pdf

Diaz, Eleanor. 2016. "Immigrants Overcome Obstacles with Library Support." *Programming Librarian*, July 14, 2016. Accessed September 18, 2017. http://www .programminglibrarian.org/articles/immigrants-overcome-obstacles-lib rary-support

Faulkner, Canaan. Personal communication with the author, October 2016. Public Relations Manager, Grandview Heights Public Library.

Ferdman, Glenn. Interview by the author, February 22, 2017. Director, Somerville Public Library.

Gates, Daryl F. 1979. *Special Order #40*, Office of the Chief of Police, November 27, 1979. Accessed September 18, 2017. http://assets.lapdonline.org/assets/pdf /SO_40.pdf

Gladwell, Malcolm. 2000. *The Tipping Point*. New York: Little Brown.

Global Talent Idaho. n.d. A "About Global Talent Idaho." Accessed November 12, 2017. http://globaltalentidaho.org/about-global-talent-idaho/

Global Talent Idaho. n.d. B "For Employers." Accessed December 2, 2017. http://globaltalentidaho.org/employers/

Gordon, Michelle. Personal communication with the author, February–August 2017. Community Librarian, Fresno County Public Library.

Graybill, Jeremy. Personal communication with the author, June 2017. Marketing + Online Engagement Director, Multnomah County Public Library.

Huertas, Adriana (Ady). Personal communication with the author, May 2016. Branch Manager, Logan Heights Branch Library, San Diego Public Library.

Hyte, Heidi. 2008. "What's the Difference: ESL, EFL, ESOL, ELL, and ESP?" Accessed September 18, 2017. http://www.esltrail.com/2008/02/whats-difference-esl-efl-esol-ell-and.html

Idaho Office for Refugees. n.d. "About Refugees in Idaho." Accessed September 18, 2017. http://www.idahorefugees.org/refugees-in-idaho.html

Ilsdefonso, Madeleine (Maddy). Interview by the author, April 28, 2017. Senior Librarian, Office of Enrichment and Empowerment, Department of Lifelong Learning, Los Angeles Public Library.

Indianapolis Public Library. n.d. "Sister City Exchange." Accessed November 12, 2017. http://www.indypl.org/sistercities/

Internal Revenue Service. n.d. "Immigration Terms and Definitions Involving Aliens." Accessed September 18, 2017. http://www.irs.gov/individuals/international-taxpayers/immigration-terms-and-definitions-involving-aliens

Izraeli, Dr. Elena. Interview by Eleanor Diaz. 2016. "Immigrants Overcome Obstacles with Library Support." *Programming Librarian*, July 14, 2016. Accessed September 18, 2017.

Izraeli, Dr. Elena. Personal communication with the author, August 2017. Leader of the ELL Newcomer's Discussion Group, Rochester Hills Public Library.

Jakubowski, Mary Jean. Via personal communication from Dawn Peters with the author, May 2016 and March 2017. Director, Buffalo & Erie County Public Library.

Johnson, Cristina (Cris). Personal communication with the author, September 2017. Family Learning Center Coordinator, Seventrees Branch, San José Public Library.

Jones, Daniel. 2015. "The 36 Questions that Lead to Love," *The New York Times*, January 9, 2015. Accessed November 12, 2017. https://nyti.ms/2jAhy7m

Journee, Mike. Interview by the author, August 16, 2017. Director of Communications, Office of the Mayor, City of Boise.

Kallenbach, Silja, and Andy Nash. 2016. *Adult Education and Immigrant Integration: Lessons Learned from the Networks for Integrating New Americans Initiative.* World Education, Inc., in partnership with Community Science, IMPRINT, National Partnership for New Americans, Network Impact, Inc., Welcoming America, Inc. 2016.

Kelley-Chase, Sarah, Interview by the author, July 10, 2017, and personal communication with the author, May 2016 and July–August 2017. Branch Manager, Library! at Bown Crossing, Boise Public Library.

Koerber, Jennifer. 2016 A. "Celebration and Integration," *Library Journal*, June 13, 2016. Accessed November 26, 2017. http://lj.libraryjournal.com/2016/06/library-services/celebration-integration-public-services/

Koerber, Jennifer. 2016 B. "It's Electric!" One Cool Thing column, *Library Journal*, November 18, 2016. Accessed November 12, 2017. http://lj.libraryjournal .com/2016/11/opinion/one-cool-thing/its-electric-one-cool-thing/

Koerber, Jennifer. 2016 C. "Working Toward Change," *Library Journal*, September 1, 2016. Accessed November 12, 2017. http://lj.libraryjournal.com/2016/09 /public-services/working-toward-change-workforce-development/

Koerber, Jennifer. 2017. "Meaningful Measures: Outcome Measures and Assessment," *Library Journal*, June 15, 2017. Accessed November 12, 2017. http://lj .libraryjournal.com/2017/06/library-services/meaningful-measures-asse ssment/

Koester, Amy. Personal communication with the author, June–July 2017. Youth and Family Program Supervisor, Skokie Public Library.

Koppel, PhD, Meg Shope. Personal communication with the author, July 2016. Chief Research Officer, Philadelphia Works.

Leonard, David. 2017. "A Message from President David Leonard," February 10, 2017. Accessed November 12, 2017. http://www.bpl.org/press/2017/02/10/a -message-from-president-david-leonard-to-the-boston-public-library -community/

Leonard, David. Personal communication with the author, April 2017. President, Boston Public Library.

Los Angeles Public Library. n.d. "Job and Career Center WorkSource Portal at the Los Angeles Public Library FAQ." Accessed November 12, 2017. http:// www.lapl.org/sites/default/files/FAQ%20for%20Central%20LibraryPortal -Johnathon%20Davis%202017.pdf

Maier, Sophie. Interview by the author, March 31, 2017, and personal communication with the author, May 2016–April 2017. Immigrant Services/Outreach Librarian, Iroquois Branch, Louisville Free Public Library.

Mattei, Annette. 2016. Story related via personal communication with the author, July 2016. Project Coordinator, The Paschalville Partnership, Philadelphia PA.

Mattei, Annette. 2017. "Community Catalyst: The Paschalville Partnership: A Local Library Leads Organizations in Assisting Job Seekers" IMLS UpNext blog. Accessed September 23, 2017. https://www.imls.gov/news-events /upnext-blog/2017/01/community-catalyst-paschalville-partnership-local -library-leads

McDonnell, Ryan. Via personal communication from Canaan Faulkner with the author, October 2016. Director, Grandview Heights Public Library.

McGovern, Sheryl. Personal communication with the author, June–July 2017. Director, Cedar Falls Public Library.

McNeil, Eileen. Via personal communication from Canaan Faulkner with the author, October 2016. Youth Services Manager, Grandview Heights Public Library.

Moguel, Alicia, Interview by the author, April 28, 2017, and personal communication with the author, May 2016–September 2017. Principal Librarian/Associate Director, Department of Lifelong Learning, Los Angeles Public Library.

Multnomah County Library. n.d. "Intercambio/Language Exchange." Accessed November 12, 2017. http://multcolib.org/events/intercambio-language -exchange

Muñoz, Cecelia, and León Rodríguez. 2015. *Strengthening Communities by Welcoming All Residents: Federal Action Plan on Immigrant and Refugee Integration.* Washington, DC: White House Task Force on New Americans. April 2015.

NACES. n.d. "About Us." Accessed December 2, 2017. http://www.naces.org/about.html

Naficy, Homa, Interview by the author, July 6, 2017, and personal communication with the author, May 2016–July 2017. Executive Director of The American Place, Hartford Public Library.

NGen Fellows. 2014. "Strategies for Talent Diversity: A Proposal for Improving the Racial and Ethnic Diversity at Nonprofit Organizations Across the Sector," report by the 2013–2014 American Express NGen Fellows, convened by Independent Sector. July 2014. Accessed November 13, 2017. http://www.independentsector.org/resource/2013-american-express-ngen-fellows-project-strategies-for-talent-diversity/

Nielsen, Victoria. Personal communication with the author, August 2017. Legal Director, Immigrant Justice Corps.

Noor, Moina. Interview by the author, August 1, 2017. Norwalk Public Library board member and member of Al Madany Islamic Center of Norwalk.

Oatis, Vicki. Interview by the author, July 31, 2017. Director of Youth Library Services, Norwalk Public Library.

Ocotillo Library & Workforce Literacy Center. n.d. Events pages, Ocotillo Library & Workforce Literacy Center, Phoenix Public Library. Accessed Spring 2016. http://www.phoenixpubliclibrary.org/Locations/Pages/Ocotillo.aspx. No longer available online

Office of Legal Access Programs, U.S. Department of Justice. Updated January 2017. *Recognition and Accreditation Program: Frequently Asked Questions.* Accessed September 18, 2017. https://www.justice.gov/sites/default/files/pages/attachments/2017/07/25/olap_ra_faqs_20170531.pdf

Peters, Dawn. Personal communication with the author, May 2016 and March 2017. Assistant Deputy Director of Public Services, Buffalo & Erie County Public Library.

Piantigini, Catherine. Interview by the author, February 22, 2017. Deputy Director for Libraries, Somerville Public Library.

Plainlanguage.gov. n.d. Accessed September 18, 2017.
A—http://www.plainlanguage.gov/howto/quickreference/checklist.cfm
B—http://www.plainlanguage.gov/howto/quickreference/weblist.cfm

Principles of Universal Design. 1997. *The Principles of Universal Design, Version 2.0.* The Center for Universal Design. Raleigh, NC: North Carolina State University. Accessed September 18, 2017. https://projects.ncsu.edu/www/ncsu/design/sod5/cud/about_ud/udprinciples.htm

ProBonoProject. n.d. About page. Accessed November 12, 2017. http://www.probonoproject.org/about/

Pyko, Marie. Personal communication with the author, July 2017. Director of Public Services, Topeka & Shawnee County Public Library.

Queens Public Library. n.d. Mission page. Accessed November 12, 2017. http://www.queenslibrary.org/about-us/mission-statement

Raison, Eva. Personal communication with the author, May 2016. Coordinator of Immigrant Services, Brooklyn Public Library.

Refugee Act of 1980. 1980. Public Law 96-212, 96th Congress, 2nd Session, U.S. Government Printing Office, 1980. Accessed September 18, 2017. http://www.gpo.gov/fdsys/pkg/STATUTE-94/pdf/STATUTE-94-Pg102.pdf

Rochester Hills (MN) Public Library. 2017. "ELL Newcomer's Book Group" program description. Accessed December 2, 2017, via link to calendar listed on http://www.rhpl.org/i-am/a-recent-immigrant/recent-immigrant-resources

San José Public Library. n.d. A "ESL Class—Beginner Level" at Dr. Roberto Cruz Alum Rock Branch Library. Accessed November 12, 2017. http://events.sjpl.org/event/english_as_a_second_language_esl_classes_pre-registration_required

San José Public Library. n.d. B "ESL Class Level 1 Beginning Clear Speech Red Book 1" at Seventrees Branch Library. Accessed November 12, 2017. http://events.sjpl.org/event/esl_class_advanced_level_reading

San José Public Library. n.d. C "ESL Class Level 5 Advance [sic] Reading, Reading Concepts 4" at Seventrees Branch Library. Accessed November 12, 2017. http://events.sjpl.org/event/esl_class_level_5_advance-_learn_real_american_english_thru_poplular_music

San José Public Library. n.d. D Mission & Vision Statement page. Accessed November 12, 2017. http://www.sjpl.org/mission

San José Public Library. n.d. E "PAR Tutor Resources." Accessed September 18, 2017. https://www.sjpl.org/partutorresources

Sister City International. n.d. "What is a Sister City?" Accessed November 12, 2017. http://www.sistercities.org/what-sister-city

Stalder, Kathleen. Personal communication with the author, August 2017. Acquisitions and Technical Services Assistant Supervisor for Collection Development, Boise Public Library.

Stewart, Helen. Personal communication with the author, August 2017. Literacy Coordinator, Schaumburg Township District Library.

Tashjian, Karisa. Personal communication with the author, May 2016. Director of RIFLI and Director of Education at Providence Public Library.

Tates, MyTesha, Personal communication with the author, July 2016. Community Engagement Manager, Houston Public Library.

Thompson, Erin. Personal communication with the author, June 2017. Technology Librarian, Cedar Falls Public Library.

Torres-Springer, Maria and Nisha Agarwal. n.d. *Unlocking Potential: Empowering New York City's Immigrant Entrepreneurs*. New York, NY: NYC Small Business Services. n.d. but possibly 2014. Accessed December 2, 2017 via link at http://nyc.gov/immigrantbusinesses. http://www1.nyc.gov/assets/sbs/downloads/pdf/about/reports/ibi_report.pdf

US Conference of Mayors Resolution, 85th Annual Meeting, June 2017. Accessed September 18, 2017. https://www.usmayors.org/the-conference/resolutions/?category=a0F6100000BKCMIEA5&meeting=85th%20Annual%20Meeting

Usability.gov. n.d. Accessed September 18, 2017. https://www.usability.gov/what-and-why/usability-evaluation.html

USCIS. n.d. A "Citizenship Corners." Accessed September 18, 2017. https://www.uscis.gov/citizenship/organizations/libraries/citizenship-corners

USCIS. n.d. B "Civics and Citizenship Toolkit." Accessed December 2, 2017. https://www.uscis.gov/citizenship/organizations/civics-and-citizenship-toolkit

USCIS. n.d. C "Glossary." Accessed September 18, 2017. https://www.uscis.gov
    /tools/glossaryUSCIS. n.d. D *USCIS Policy Manual*, Volume 12—Citizenship &
    Naturalization, Part J—Oath of Allegiance, Chapter 5—Administrative
    Naturalization Ceremonies. Accessed November 12, 2017. http://www
    .uscis.gov/policymanual/HTML/PolicyManual-Volume12-PartJ-Chapter5
    .html

Vestal, Joan. Personal communication with the author, August 2017. Information
    Services Librarian (retired), Boise Public Library.

Welcoming America. n.d. A "FAQs." Accessed September 28, 2017. https://www
    .welcomingamerica.org/about/faq

Welcoming America. n.d. B "What Is Welcoming Week?" Accessed September 28,
    2017. http://www.welcomingamerica.org/programs/welcoming-week

Wisniewski, Michelle. Personal communication with the author, August 2017.
    Oakland Talking Book Service Librarian, Rochester Hills Public Library.

INDEX

ABOUT THE AUTHOR

JENNIFER KOERBER is a consultant, writer, and trainer working in the intersection of technology, everyday life, and libraries. She held a variety of roles during her 17 years at the Boston Public Library and is currently the training project manager for Harvard Library's implementation of the Alma (Ex Libris) unified resource management system. Jennifer is co-author of *Emerging Technologies: A Primer for Librarians* (Rowman & Littlefield, May 2015, with Michael P. Sauers) and has written extensively for *Library Journal* on technology and public service in libraries.